CONTEMPORARY WOMEN SCIENTISTS

A M E R I C A N
P R O F I L E S

CONTEMPORARY WOMEN SCIENTISTS

■

Lisa Yount

Facts On File®

AN INFOBASE HOLDINGS COMPANY

Contemporary Women Scientists

Facts On File, Inc.
460 Park Avenue South
New York NY 10016

Library of Congress Cataloging-in-Publication Data
Yount, Lisa.
    Contemporary women scientists / Lisa Yount.
    p. cm. — (American profiles)
    Includes bibliographical references and index.
    ISBN 0-8160-2895-8
    1. Women scientists—United States—Biography. 2. Women in science—United States—History—20th century. I. Title. II. Series: American profiles (Facts on File, Inc.)
    Q130.Y65 1994
    509.2'273—dc20
    [B]   93-26821

A British CIP catalogue record for this book is available from the British Library.

Facts On File books are available at special discounts when purchased in bulk quantities for businesses, associations, institutions or sales promotions. Please call our Special Sales Department in New York at 212/683-2244 or 800/322-8755.

Text design by Ron Monteleone
Cover design by Ron Monteleone
Composition by Facts On File, Inc./Grace M. Ferrara
Manufactured by the Maple-Vail Book Manufacturing Group
Printed in the United States of America

10 9 8 7 6 5 4 3 2 1

To all the women scientists in this book
To all the women scientists not in this book
To all the future women scientists who
will read this book

Contents

Acknowledgments

I would like to thank Gertrude Elion, Eugenie Clark, Jewel Cobb, Vera Rubin, Candace Pert, and Flossie Wong-Staal for their time and courtesy in letting me interview them for this book. I also thank Robert G. Sachs of the Enrico Fermi Institute for reading the Maria Mayer chapter, Harry Henderson and Hal Heydt for giving me technical advice on the Grace Hopper chapter, and Katherine MacFarlane for providing the line illustrations and diagrams.

Introduction

Women in science have come a long way during this century—or have they?

The careers of the 10 women described in this book suggest that in some ways the answer is yes. No university today would make a woman take classes in a room separate from male students, as Helen Taussig had to do in the 1920s. No employer would dare to tell a female job applicant that she cannot be hired because she would be a "distraction" to male employees, as the head of one laboratory told Gertrude Elion in the 1930s. Rules against an institution's hiring both a husband and a wife are unlikely to keep a woman scientist unsalaried for most of her career, as happened to Maria Mayer. In short, obvious discrimination against a woman scientist because of her gender has become rare. Most of the women in this book encountered it only very early in their careers or else not at all.

The number of women entering careers in science has increased greatly as well. In 1930, when Helen Taussig took over the children's heart clinic at Johns Hopkins, women scientists were so rare as to be almost freaks. They were still uncommon in the early 1970s, when Candace Pert and Flossie Wong-Staal, the book's youngest scientists, began their careers. Now, however, there are almost as many women science students as men. According to a survey reported in *Science* magazine, 40 percent of the bachelor's degrees in chemistry given in 1988 went to women. Thirty-eight percent of medical students and the same percentage of undergraduate mathematics majors today are women.

There, unfortunately, the good news stops. Women in American science still do not have the same opportunities as men. The six scientists interviewed for this book all agreed that the position of women in science has improved during the 50-year span of their collective careers, but it still has a long way to go. Statistical studies such as those reported in *Science* magazine's special "Women in Science" issue (March 13, 1992) bear out their impressions. The problems women face today are subtle compared to those of their forebears, but that just makes the problems harder to fight.

The number of women in science drops sharply as one moves up the career ladder. Women "leak out of the pipeline" at every step. In Candace Pert's field, neuroscience (the study of the brain), for example, *Science* reports that 45 percent of graduate students entering the field are women. However, the figure is only 38 percent for those receiving Ph.D.s and 33 percent for those doing postdoctoral studies—and that's just the beginning. Only 8 percent of full professors (the highest position) in the science departments of U.S. universities are women.

As a woman rises in the science hierarchy, she usually encounters what has been called "the glass ceiling." (This problem is not limited to science, or to women; minorities of both sexes also face it.) The term refers to the fact that there is seldom an official policy that prevents a woman from becoming, say, the head of an academic department—but it just does not happen. "At the higher levels, things are still ridiculously blocked," Candace Pert says.

Women run into "glass" barriers at every step of their careers. As young scientists, they have trouble finding older scientists to be their mentors. A mentor guides a scientist's early career and "see[s] that good things happen and bad things don't happen," as Vera Rubin puts it. When women advance, if they work for a university, they are likely to be pushed into jobs that do not lead to tenure (permanent employment). If they do get a "tenure-track" position, they may have trouble showing the research performance that tenure approval requires because, for example, they are less likely to be asked to speak at scientific meetings and less likely to be published in (or even submit their research papers to) major science journals. They may fail to get a vote of approval for tenure if even one man on the approval committee does not want to work with a woman. Even after women get tenure, they are less likely than men to be appointed to the powerful committees that run scientific meetings or control university budgets. Similar glass ceilings exist in private research institutions and in industry. Women often receive unequal pay as well as unequal chances for advancement.

The problem seems to be that many men, especially older men in positions of power, still see women as outsiders, and they take conscious or unconscious steps to keep them that way. Margrete S. Klein, director of women's programs at the National Science Foundation, says that "the old-boy network . . . [is] still very much in place." Similarly, Candace Pert calls the prestigious, government-run National Institutes of Health (NIH) "an old boys' club." Women may have an easier time advancing in science in the future when successful women, like those in this book, break through the "glass ceiling" and then lean down to help others. "I hope that I can . . . contribute to making things change for other women in science by . . . being in positions that can make decisions," Flossie Wong-Staal says. Several groups of women scientists have also tried to balance the "old boys' club" by forming their own networks and mentoring programs. Candace Pert helped to found an organization called Women in Neuroscience, for example. *Science* reports that a group of women in engineering and computer science have formed a computerized network that they call Systers, from a combination of *sisters* and *system*.

Women in science face a second major problem in addition to the glass ceiling. This is the potential conflict between career and family life.

One way around the conflict, of course, is not to have a family. Many women scientists of the 19th and early 20th centuries became what Candace Pert calls "science nuns" because most people—often including the women themselves—believed that a woman could not handle both a family and a demanding career. Some people still held this view as late as the 1940s, when a department chairman at a prestigious university told Eugenie Clark that he was reluctant to take her on as a Ph.D. student because "I can tell by looking at you that you're probably going to get married, have kids, and . . . not pursue a career."

Clark did get married and have children—four of them. She also pursued a very successful science career. In this she is typical of the scientists in this book. Of the 10 women profiled here, only two (Helen Taussig and Gertrude Elion) did not marry, and Elion remained single mostly because her fiancé died. Only one of the eight women who married (Grace Hopper) did not have children. These women's lives suggest that contemporary women scientists feel no need to choose between a family and a science career.

This does not mean that combining career and family is easy. It may be significant that the marriages of five of the eight married scientists in this book ended in divorce (although the role of career conflicts in those divorces is unknown). One problem arises when a woman scientist marries another scientist, as many (including six of the eight married scientists in this book) do. This difficulty has been called "the two-body problem," after a famous problem in mathematics. What should a scientific couple do if husband and wife receive job offers from companies or universities in different cities? Should they live apart or commute, perhaps over long distances? Or should one or the other—and which one?—turn down a job or accept a less prestigious position so the couple can be together?

There used to be only one answer. Maria Mayer went where Joe Mayer went, even though doing so kept her from being paid for her work. Vera Rubin followed her husband to Cornell, with what she calls "very little thought," even though that university offered her a poor opportunity for graduate work in astronomy. Today, however, mutual love, respect, and willingness to compromise help scientific couples work out more creative solutions to the "two-body problem." Rubin, for example, has described how she and her husband coordinate their travel plans so that both can go to science meetings.

The two-body problem becomes more complex when more bodies—those of children—are added to the family group. The "three-ring circus" Vera Rubin describes for the time when she was juggling two young children and her Ph.D. studies is typical. Succeeding at the "circus" requires determination and stamina. It also requires a supportive husband, parents who will help with child care (Vera Rubin's parents and Eugenie Clark's mother and stepfather both did this), or "spending a major percentage of your income on help," as Candace Pert (along with Maria Mayer and Flossie Wong-Staal) did. The challenge becomes even greater when a woman scientist divorces and has to raise children as a single parent, as happened to Jewel Cobb, Eugenie Clark, Candace Pert, and Flossie Wong-Staal during part of their careers.

Nonetheless, all seven of the women with children have expressed great pride and happiness in their families. "My kids are great," Candace Pert says of her three. "I am very glad that I . . . have my daughters," Flossie Wong-Staal agrees. "I think life would be . . . a lot less complete without children." Maria Mayer called having children "a tremendous experience." The children, in turn, may have benefited from having mothers with such interesting lives, even if that meant seeing less of them. It seems significant that many of these women's children (including all four of Vera Rubin's) have followed their mothers into science careers.

When asked what qualities a young woman planning to be a scientist should have, the six scientists interviewed for this book mention willingness to work hard, faith in one's ideas, and persistence in the face of discouragement—persistence above all. As Vera Rubin says, girls interested in science must "absolutely not give up, . . . just not let anyone discourage them, . . . ignore all the advice they get which is negative."

A career in science obviously is challenging at best, especially for a woman who chooses to combine it with raising a family. Why should a woman want to take on such struggles and sacrifices? What are the rewards of a scientific career?

Whether given in the interviews done for this book or in response to questions from other interviewers, these 10 woman scientists' answers are remarkably similar. Most center on one word: *fun.* "That was the fun—seeing it work out," Maria Mayer told an interviewer, explaining why the moment of imagining her shell theory meant more to her than the fact that she later won a Nobel Prize for it. "We've got to really show them [young people] . . . how much fun it is . . ., how you really don't want to see the weekend come," Gertrude Elion says. Vera Rubin adds, "Doing astronomy is incredibly great fun." It is interesting that in connection with her description of Maria Mayer, author Joan Dash says that men scientists make exactly the same response when asked why they like science: "It's fun; we love it because it's fun."

Quite simply, then, the secret of these 10 women's success—often in the face of subtle or not-so-subtle obstacles and enormous demands on their time and energy—is surely that they are doing what they enjoy above all else. Most of them have gone on doing it long past retirement age. The "fun" they get from science never stops.

If science is fun for you, too, don't let anyone or anything stop you from making a career of it. As Helen M. Free, president of the American Chemical Society, says, "If you want it all, you'll find a way." The 10 women in this book did. All became first-class scientists while leading full personal lives. There's no reason you can't do the same.

Helen Brooke Taussig
(1898–1986)

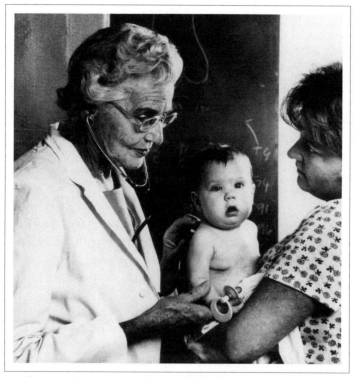

Helen Brooke Taussig with one of her "little crossword puzzles."
Taussig invented an operation that saved the lives of babies
born with heart defects.
(Courtesy Alan Mason Chesney Archives of the
Johns Hopkins Medical Institutions)

A baby is born, and its parents are thrilled. It is chubby and
healthy looking. For the first year of the child's life, all goes
well—but then things begin to change. Whenever the child plays
hard, it becomes out of breath. Its lips and fingernails take on a
bluish color.

1

The problem gets worse as the child grows older. The child fails to grow normally. It gasps for breath and may even faint after the slightest exercise. The blue color grows darker and spreads to most of the child's skin. Very likely the child will die before it is 12 years old.

Helen Taussig saw children like this often in her pediatric cardiology clinic at Johns Hopkins Medical School in Baltimore, Maryland. They had been born with defective hearts. (Pediatrics is the branch of medicine that treats children, and cardiology is the study of the heart.) They were called "blue babies" because of the color of their skin.

For years Taussig could do little except watch most of her young patients die. But then, in the early 1940s, she had an idea for an operation that might help them. Carried out by a skilled surgeon, this operation allowed most "blue babies" to grow up and live normal lives. It was only one of the ways that Helen Taussig saved the lives and health of children during her long career.

Helen Brooke Taussig was born on May 24, 1898, in Cambridge, Massachusetts. She was the youngest of four children. Her father, Frank Taussig, was a world-famous economist who taught at Harvard University. Her mother, Edith, died when Helen was about 11 years old.

Frank Taussig's father had been a well-known doctor, so perhaps it was not surprising that Helen Taussig developed an interest in medicine. She began showing her interest soon after she went to Radcliffe, the women's college attached to Harvard, in 1917. She transferred to the University of California at Berkeley after two years and graduated in 1921.

Taussig wanted to go to medical school, but most medical schools did not accept women in those days. Harvard, Taussig's first choice, was one of them. School officials told her she could attend certain classes there but could not be granted a degree.

Harvard's refusal to consider her simply made Taussig more determined. She took what classes she could, even though that meant sitting in a corner by herself during lectures and working in a separate room when students studied tissues of the human body under the microscope.

Taussig took other classes at Boston University's medical school. One of these was anatomy, or the structure of the body.

Alexander Begg was her anatomy teacher. One day Begg startled Taussig by shoving a beef heart into her hand. "Here," he said. "It wouldn't hurt you to become interested in a major organ of the body." That was Helen Taussig's introduction to cardiology.

Impressed with Taussig's ability, Begg recommended that she apply to the medical school at Johns Hopkins. The school was excellent, and it accepted women. Taussig transferred to Johns Hopkins in 1923 and received her M.D. degree in 1927.

Taussig did her internship, or year of practical medical training, in pediatrics at Johns Hopkins. She also worked at the hospital's Heart Station. In 1930 Edwards Park, the medical school's chairman of pediatrics, put her in charge of the new pediatric cardiology clinic he had started.

Helen Taussig became expert at identifying different heart problems in the children who came to the clinic. Most doctors made this kind of diagnosis, or identification of a medical problem, partly by listening to the heart through a stethoscope. The stethoscope magnifies the sounds that the heart makes when it pumps. Taussig's hearing, however, had been partly impaired by illness when she was a child. Instead of her ears, therefore, she used her hands and her eyes. She found she could learn a great deal by feeling a child's chest and by studying the chest's shape and its movements as the child struggled to breathe.

Taussig also used a machine called a fluoroscope, which was new at the time. The fluoroscope worked something like an X ray, projecting shadowy images of the heart, lungs, and major blood vessels onto a screen. Taussig could look at the screen and watch a child's heart beat. Turning the child at different angles, she got a clear idea of the size and shape of the heart and nearby blood vessels. She became skilled at matching what she saw in the fluoroscope with the defects that were known from examining hearts after death and with the particular signs of illness that the children showed.

In the late 1930s Taussig became especially interested in children who had been born with heart problems. The "blue babies" were among these. Taussig knew that these children's blue skin color meant that their bodies were not getting enough oxygen.

All body tissues need oxygen. The lungs take in oxygen during inhalation, and the blood picks up this gas when it circulates through the lungs. Hemoglobin, the pigment that colors the blood, carries oxygen to the body tissues.

3

Hemoglobin is bright red when it is carrying oxygen. That is why blood in the arteries, the tubes or vessels that bring oxygen-carrying blood from the heart to the rest of the body, looks red. This red blood gives the skin of light-skinned people its pink color. After blood has given up oxygen in the body, however, it turns bluish. For this reason, blood in the veins, the vessels that carry blood back to the heart, looks blue. In the blue babies, the blood in both arteries and veins was blue because it contained very little oxygen.

Most of the blue babies had been born with a group of four heart and blood vessel defects. Their condition was called tetralogy of Fallot. (*Tetra-* means four; Fallot was a French physician who had described the defects.) One defect was in the pulmonary artery, the artery that takes blood from the lower right chamber of the heart (right ventricle) to the lungs. The part of the artery just outside the ventricle was much narrower than it should have been, so very little blood could flow through it.

A second defect was in the heart itself. The heart's right and left sides are normally divided by a solid wall of muscle. In babies with tetralogy of Fallot, however, this wall had a hole in it. When the right ventricle tried to pump blood into the lungs, some of the blood was pushed through the hole into the left ventricle instead.

Taussig was the first to combine the knowledge of these defects, which Fallot and others had seen when they examined hearts of children who had died, with the information given by the children's blue color. She realized that the children's main problem was that very little blood was reaching their lungs. This meant that the blood could not pick up its cargo of life-giving oxygen. The children died, not from the defects themselves, but from lack of oxygen.

Another birth defect that Taussig often saw was called a ductus arteriosus. A child's lungs do not work before it is born; it gets oxygen from its mother's blood. In unborn children a small duct or shunt (connecting vessel) joins the pulmonary artery to the aorta, the main artery that carries blood to the body. This lets the blood bypass the lungs.

Normally this shunt closes off at birth. In some children, however, it does not. Because the blood pressure in the aorta is higher than that in the pulmonary artery after birth, extra blood from the aorta is forced into the pulmonary artery. As a result, the lungs get too much blood, under too high a pressure. This damages the delicate lung tissue. Some unlucky children were born with both a ductus arteriosus and tetralogy of Fallot.

In 1939 a doctor named Robert Gross, at Boston Children's Hospital, developed an operation that tied off or closed the ductus arteriosus. Most children with this defect recovered their health after the operation. Helen Taussig noticed, however, that children who also had tetralogy of Fallot did not. Instead, they often became worse or died. The same thing happened when such children had a ductus arteriosus that closed up on its own after birth.

Taussig came to realize that the ductus arteriosus actually helped children with tetralogy of Fallot. It sent blood to their lungs by a route that bypassed their defective heart and pulmonary artery. Taussig began to wonder: If an operation could close a ductus arteriosis, why couldn't another operation make an artificial one?

Taussig looked for a surgeon who would try her idea. She first talked to Gross, the man who had become famous for doing operations to close the ductus, but he was not interested. Luckily Alfred Blalock, chief of surgery at Johns Hopkins, offered a more sympathetic ear. Taussig first spoke to him about the idea of making an artificial ductus in the fall of 1943.

Blalock was not afraid to take chances, and he thought Taussig's idea might work. Indeed, he had already performed a similar operation on dogs. In this operation he connected the subclavian artery, which carried blood to the front of the body (to the arms in humans), to the pulmonary artery. He had done the operation to make an animal model in which he could study the lung damage caused by an open ductus arteriosus.

Blalock and his assistant, an African-American man named Vivian Thomas, perfected the operation by trying it on over 200 dogs. They then felt ready to try it on a human "blue baby." They believed that the child's lungs would not be harmed by the extra blood because the lungs got so little blood from the normal source, the right side of the heart.

Eileen Saxon was the first baby to receive the new Blalock-Taussig operation. She was 11 months old and in such poor health that she had to live in an oxygen tent. Blalock operated on Eileen on November 29, 1944. Eileen's mother later told an interviewer, "When I was allowed to see Eileen for the first time [after the operation], it was like a miracle. . . . I was beside myself with happiness."

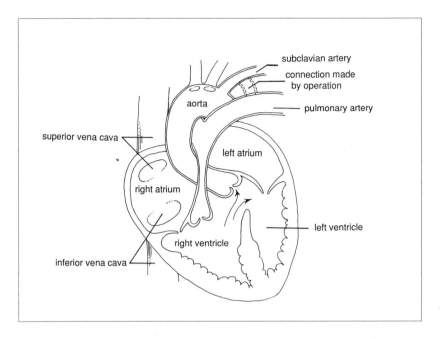

The Blalock-Taussig "blue baby" operation. By joining the subclavian artery to the pulmonary artery, the operation sent extra blood to the children's lungs.
(Courtesy Katherine MacFarlane)

Blalock did two more operations in February 1945. Taussig wrote about her feelings while watching the second of these. "That operation was on a small, utterly miserable, six-year-old boy who . . . was no longer able to walk. . . . When the clamps were released [after Blalock had joined the blood vessels] the anesthesiologist said suddenly, 'He's a lovely color now!' I walked around to the head of the table and saw his normal, pink lips. From that moment the child was healthy, happy, and active."

The "blue baby" operations saved the lives of more than just the 12,000 children who eventually received them. They showed that even seriously ill children could survive such major surgery. This encouraged doctors to develop operations that could help people with other kinds of heart problems. A famous surgeon later said that Blalock's and Taussig's accomplishments "prompted surgeons to venture where they had not dared to venture previously.

The result is much of present-day cardiac surgery." The Blalock-Taussig operation continued to be done until heart surgery became advanced enough to let the hole in the heart and the defective pulmonary artery be repaired directly.

The dramatic, life-saving operations made both Blalock and Taussig famous. Most of the fame, however, went to Blalock at first. Taussig was hurt by this, but her hurt was eased by the fact that she did not really like being a media star. She just wanted to get back to the beloved children whom she called her "little crossword puzzles." They now came to her clinic from all over the world. She often stayed there until 9 o'clock at night to care for them.

With the blue babies came young doctors, eager to learn about the operation and the new specialty of pediatric cardiology that Taussig had almost single-handedly invented. Taussig found an additional career in training them. She became professor of pediatrics, Johns Hopkins's first woman full professor, in 1959.

Something Helen Taussig heard from one of these doctors led her to make headlines for a second time. The doctor was Alois Beuren, a West German, who visited Taussig in January 1962. "We had dinner together," Taussig remembered later, "and he began to tell me about all the limbless babies being born in Germany. He mentioned that some investigators had implicated a drug."

The babies were suffering from a birth defect called phocomelia, which means "seal limbs." In the most severely deformed ones, the arms—and sometimes the legs as well—were missing completely. Hands and feet were attached directly to the trunk, like seal flippers. Some of the children had internal defects as well.

Phocomelia had been so rare that only 15 cases had been reported in Germany between 1949 and 1958. In 1959, however, 16 cases of phocomelia were reported. In 1960 there were 124.

A German doctor, Widukind Lenz, began to suspect that the sudden increase in phocomelia might be connected to a popular sleeping medicine called Contergan. The drug's chemical name was thalidomide. Contergan had become widely used in Germany in the late 1950s, just before the phocomelia births started increasing. Doctors often recommended it for pregnant women because it controlled their daily nausea, or morning sickness.

Lenz and other doctors asked the mothers of the "seal-limb" babies what medicines they had taken during their pregnancy. Over half of the women said they had used Contergan during the first months of the pregnancy. This did not prove that the drug had caused the

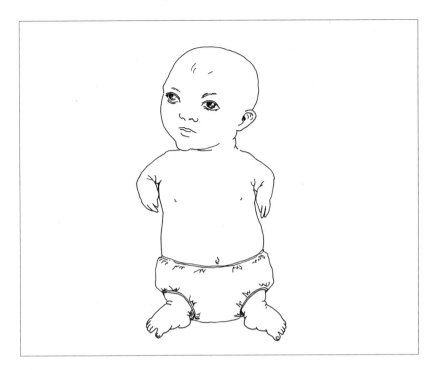

Baby with "seal-limb" birth defects caused by thalidomide. Helen Taussig alerted doctors in the United States to the dangers of this popular sleeping medicine.
(Courtesy Katherine MacFarlane)

defects, but suspicion was so strong that the company that made Contergan stopped selling it in November 1961.

Many doctors would have regarded Beuren's story simply as a medical oddity or, at most, "not my problem, thank goodness." Not Helen Taussig. Indeed, she later accused herself of being "slow on the uptake" in reacting to Beuren's report because "I didn't realize until the next morning that I had to go abroad to find out for myself about this drug and the deformities it caused."

Taussig arrived in Europe on February 1 and stayed for six weeks. She visited clinics in Germany and in Britain, where thalidomide also had been sold. She saw the seal-limb babies and talked to doctors who suspected thalidomide as the cause of the defects.

When Taussig returned, she spoke to Frances Kelsey, a medical doctor working for the government's Food and Drug Administration (FDA). Kelsey had been reviewing an American drug company's request to sell thalidomide in the United States. Taussig's report confirmed Kelsey's doubts about the drug.

Kelsey withdrew the drug from testing at once and later banned it completely. Meanwhile Taussig, hoping to reach doctors who had been given thalidomide to test in their patients, made a speech about the drug's dangers in an extra session of the April 11 meeting of the American College of Physicians.

Taussig pointed out that the thalidomide horror story reflected a general danger. "All new drugs which circulate through the bloodstream should be screened for their effect on the offspring of pregnant animals," she wrote in June 1962. "Our Food and Drug Act . . . should be strengthened." Voters and Congress agreed. Congress passed a new law that required more thorough testing before drugs could be sold. The law went into effect in February 1963. Thus Taussig's action helped to prevent future birth defects, not only from thalidomide, but from other medications as well.

Helen Taussig retired from Johns Hopkins in July 1963, but she did not really change her schedule. She still came to the cardiology clinic on most days. She still wrote scientific papers; indeed, 41 of her 100 papers were written after her "retirement." She still traveled around the country speaking about medical subjects and about children's health-care needs. In 1965 she became the first woman president of the American Heart Association, a large volunteer organization that sponsors research on heart disease. She also won many honorary doctorates and other awards. One was the Medal of Freedom, the highest award that the United States can give to a civilian. In 1977 a biographical article described Taussig as "probably the best-known woman physician in the world."

Helen Taussig moved to Pennsylvania in the late 1970s. She was killed in a car accident on May 21, 1986, three days before her 88th birthday.

One of the projects Taussig had pursued in her last years was a follow-up of children who had had her "blue baby" operation between 1945 and 1950. She was able to keep track of these people partly because she had developed close relationships with them. She was pleased to discover that most of them had lived to grow up and have children of their own. Furthermore, many had gone to college and had successful careers. This proved, as she pointed out in a 1975 paper, that the lack of oxygen they had suffered before the operation had not damaged their brains. This study was just one example of the mixture of scientific thoroughness and personal, caring interest that made Helen Taussig such a perfect example of what a doctor should be.

Chronology

May 24, 1898	Helen Brooke Taussig born in Cambridge
1921	graduates from University of California at Berkeley
1927	gains M.D. degree from Johns Hopkins
1930	takes charge of pediatric cardiac clinic
1943	speaks to Alfred Blalock about idea for operation to help "blue babies"
November 29, 1944	first operation done on human "blue baby"
1959	Taussig becomes professor of pediatrics, Johns Hopkins's first woman full professor
January 1962	hears about "seal-limb" birth defects possibly caused by thalidomide
February 1962	visits Europe to check out thalidomide reports
April 1962	speaks to American College of Physicians about thalidomide
March 1963	law requiring more careful drug testing goes into effect
July 1963	Taussig retires from Johns Hopkins
1965	becomes first woman president of American Heart Association
May 21, 1986	Taussig dies in automobile accident

Further Reading

"Blalock, Alfred, and Taussig, Helen Brooke." *Current Biography 1946*. Biographical sketch of both doctors, written soon after the "blue baby" operation became a success.

Davis, Goode P., Jr., and Edwards Park. *The Heart*. New York: Torstar Books, 1984. Provides background information on normal functioning and diseases of the heart; includes a one-page sketch of Taussig and her work.

"Dr. Helen Taussig, Heart Surgery Pioneer." *Journal of the American Medical Association*, August 9, 1976. Describes Taussig's life and work.

Froslid, E. Kenneth. "Helen Taussig, M.D.—Savior of Blue Babies." *Today's Health*, August 1968. Interesting account of Taussig's life and career.

"A Lady's Hand Guides Fight on Heart Disease." *Business Week*, November 20, 1965. Written when Taussig became president of the American Heart Association.

Nuland, Sherwin B. *Doctors: The Biography of Medicine*. New York: Random House, 1989. Chapter on Taussig is probably the most complete account of her life and work.

Taussig, Helen. "A Firsthand Report on What Happened in Europe." *U.S. News and World Report*, August 13, 1962. Taussig's report of her trip to investigate birth defects caused by thalidomide.

_____. "The Thalidomide Syndrome." *Scientific American*, August 1962. More detailed account of thalidomide's role in causing the birth of "seal-limb" babies.

Maria Goeppert Mayer
(1906–1972)

Maria Goeppert Mayer. Mayer's shell theory explained the arrangement of particles in the nucleus of atoms.
(Courtesy the Enrico Fermi Institute, University of Chicago)

With the ladies' brilliant skirts flaring out, a crowd of waltzers whirls around a ballroom. The dancers move in circles, each circle inside another. The pairs in some circles go around the room clockwise, in others counterclockwise. In addition, each dancing couple spins constantly, like a top. Some pairs spin clockwise, others turn counterclockwise.

With this simple picture, bringing back memories of the dancing she herself had done as a young woman in Germany, Maria

Goeppert Mayer explained to her young daughter the great discovery she had made. Mayer's "dancers" were not people but particles in the center of atoms. In a flash of insight, Mayer had grasped a fundamental truth about the way these particles were arranged. She received the Nobel Prize in physics for this insight in 1963. At the time of the award, her discovery was hailed as the greatest contribution to theoretical nuclear physics since the end of World War II.

Maria Goeppert was born on June 28, 1906, in Kattowitz (today Katowice), then a part of Germany but now in Poland. When she was four, her family moved to Göttingen, a walled German city founded in the Middle Ages. Göttingen's Georgia Augusta University was world famous, especially in mathematics. Maria's father, Friedrich Goeppert, joined the university as a professor of pediatrics, the branch of medicine that treats children. (As an adult, Maria proudly announced that "On my father's side, I am the seventh straight generation of university professor.") Maria's mother, also named Maria, loved to give parties in the Goepperts' large, flower-filled house.

The assassination that sparked World War I took place on Maria's eighth birthday. During the war years the Goepperts, like many other Germans, lived on what they could find or grow. Maria remembered many days of eating turnip soup, sometimes flavored with a pig's ear.

Maria entered Göttingen University in 1924 as a student in mathematics. At that time, Göttingen's fame in mathematics was being joined by a different kind of fame as a new group of men came there to study and teach. They included some of the brightest minds in atomic physics, the study of the newly discovered world inside the basic building blocks of matter. Among these men were several who would later win the Nobel Prize, including Max Born and the Italian Enrico Fermi.

By the turn of the century, scientists knew that atoms contained both positive and negative electrical charges. The charges canceled each other out, so individual atoms were electrically neutral. In 1911 a British scientist named Ernest Rutherford demonstrated that all the positive charge in an atom existed in a small, dense center, or nucleus. He proposed that electrons (negatively charged particles) circle or orbit an atom's nucleus much as the planets in our solar system orbit the sun.

Maria Goeppert Mayer

Soon afterward a Danish physicist, Niels Bohr, developed the quantum theory, which stated that electrons could move only in certain paths or orbits around the nucleus. Many of the physicists who came to Göttingen in the late 1920s were trying to work out the laws of quantum mechanics, the new field of study that grew out of Bohr's theory. As one of them wrote, "It became . . . clear that . . . we had stumbled upon a quite unexpected and deeply embedded layer of the secrets of Nature."

The field of quantum mechanics was "young and exciting" in those days, and Maria Goeppert was soon caught up in that excitement. One day in 1927 Max Born invited her to his physics class. Maria quickly decided that physics was even more interesting than mathematics. "Mathematics began to seem too much like puzzle solving," she said later. "Physics is puzzle solving, too, but of puzzles created by nature, not by the mind of man."

In that same year Maria's father died. Her mother began taking in boarders to make extra money. One winter day in 1928 a tall, lanky young American named Joseph Mayer knocked on the Goepperts' door. Mayer, a chemist, had come to spend a year in Göttingen after finishing his graduate studies in California. A friend had told him to get a room at the Goepperts' house because "the prettiest girl in Göttingen" lived there. Seeing slender, blonde Maria, Joe Mayer decided that his friend had been right.

Maria was quiet and reserved, while Joe was outgoing and friendly. Still, they found interests in common and soon were in love. They were married on January 19, 1930. With a little nagging from Joe and her mother, Maria finished her Ph.D. research and got her degree later that same year.

The newlywed Mayers sailed to the United States. Joe Mayer became an assistant professor of chemistry at Johns Hopkins University in Baltimore at about the same time Helen Taussig was taking over the pediatric cardiology clinic in the university's medical school. Maria Mayer, however, was taken on only as a "volunteer research associate." She was paid just a few hundred dollars a year—not to teach physics, but to write letters in German for one Johns Hopkins professor. Hopkins would not offer Mayer a faculty position, in spite of her qualifications, because of an "antinepotism" rule. This rule said that no more than one member of a family could work for the university. Many institutions had such rules, which had been made to spread out job opportunities during the Great Depression.

Mayer nonetheless continued to do research "just for the fun of doing physics." She worked mostly with her husband and one other professor. She taught them all she knew of atomic physics and quantum mechanics, which were not well known in the United States. In turn, they taught her physical chemistry—"chemistry in the sense of the facts," as Maria put it. For Maria, always a theorist, this taste of experimental science was enlightening. She was soon engaged in chemical research of her own, studying molecules in dyes.

Late in 1932 Mayer found she was pregnant. She wanted her child to have two American parents, so she became a naturalized United States citizen in the spring of 1933. The Mayers' daughter Maria Anne (Marianne) was born soon after.

Frightening changes were occurring at that same time in Maria's old homeland. Adolf Hitler, leader of the National Socialist Party (the Nazis), took control of Germany. The Nazis blamed the Jews for all of Germany's problems. One of Hitler's first acts was to pass restrictive laws against them. These laws forced some 200 Jewish professors, including many of Maria's old friends, out of their jobs.

Max Born and a number of other Jewish scientists left Germany immediately. The Fascists, a political party with ideas similar to Hitler's, had taken power in Italy, so Enrico Fermi and his Jewish wife left their homeland as well. Some of these scientific refugees went to other parts of Europe. Others went to the United States. Many of the latter came to the Mayers, who helped them find new jobs and homes.

In 1937 the Mayers started work on a book, *Statistical Mechanics,* which described the behavior of molecules. Unfortunately, at this time Joe lost his chance at tenure (the right to a permanent job at the university), which meant that he would have had to leave Johns Hopkins in two years. Columbia University immediately offered him tenure at a higher rank and salary—but there was still no paid position for Maria. The Mayers moved to New Jersey, just across the river from Columbia in New York City, after their son Peter was born in 1938.

The Mayers, along with Enrico Fermi and Niels Bohr, took part in a grim meeting in Washington, D.C., in January 1939. Bohr announced that two German scientists had just found that when atoms of the chemical element uranium are exposed to neutrons, the neutrons make the uranium nuclei split, releasing a huge amount of energy. (Physicists had learned in 1932 that the atomic nucleus contained particles called protons, which were positively charged, and neutrons, which were electrically neutral.)

Enrico Fermi's wife, Laura, wrote later that Bohr was "stooped like a man carrying a burden." Bohr's burden was that he guessed what the development of nuclear splitting, or fission, might mean. If the process released more neutrons, which could then split more uranium atoms, the resulting "chain reaction" could produce tremendous energy. The scientists tried to warn the U.S. government that nuclear fission might be used to make "an explosive that would liberate a million times as much energy per pound as any known explosive."

Angered by Adolf Hitler's invasion of several eastern European countries, France and Britain declared war on Germany in September 1939. Now the American government, concerned about the possibility that Germany might develop and use a nuclear fission bomb, heeded the scientists' warnings. In October President Franklin Roosevelt appointed the Uranium Committee, which launched a program to develop an atomic weapon. As a first step, the committee decided on December 6, 1941, to set up an experimental chain reaction at the University of Chicago. The very next day, December 7, Japan bombed the U.S. base at Pearl Harbor, Hawaii. The United States declared war on Japan, thus entering World War II.

Enrico Fermi and some of the Mayers' other scientist friends went to Chicago to work on the top-secret bomb project, which became known as the Manhattan Project. Meanwhile, Maria Mayer was asked to join a secret group at Columbia called SAM (short for Substitute Alloy Materials, a code name). The SAM group was trying to find ways to separate the isotope uranium-235 from the more abundant isotope uranium-238. (All atoms of a chemical element have the same number of protons, but different isotopes of an element have different numbers of neutrons.) Getting a supply of uranium-235 was important because only the nuclei of uranium-235 could be split by neutrons. Uranium-235 would become the fuel for the new bomb.

Mayer agreed to work for the SAM project, but the decision was a hard one. She still had friends and relatives in Germany, and she knew the United States might drop an atomic bomb there. She also disliked being unable to talk to Joe about her top-secret work.

Still, Maria Mayer hated the Nazis. She could not bear to think what would happen if Germany developed the bomb first. She also

Atomic bomb blast over Nagasaki, Japan. Maria Mayer helped to develop the bombs that ended World War II, but she wished they hadn't worked.
(Courtesy Library of Congress)

was proud to be sought after in her own right. "It was the beginning of myself standing on my own two feet as a scientist, not leaning on Joe," she said later. The project leader even offered to pay her!

In time Mayer had 20 scientists working for her. Even so, she was assigned to "side issues . . . nice, clean physics . . . [that] did not help in the separation of isotopes." Some of her work, however, did lead indirectly to advances in isotope separation that were important later in geology, chemistry, and other fields.

In August 1945 the Mayers, with Marianne and Peter, took a vacation in Nantucket, Massachusetts. They were walking along the beach on August 6 when a neighbor ran up to them. "Did you have anything to do with the atomic bomb, Professor Mayer?" she asked. (Of course, she spoke to Joe.) She had just heard that the bomb had been dropped on Hiroshima, Japan. (A second bomb was dropped on the city of Nagasaki three days later. Japan surrendered on August 14.)

Maria's first thought on hearing about the Hiroshima bomb was, "Oh, how I wish it hadn't worked!" Her second was that she could finally tell Joe everything. The Mayers sent the neighbor away and told the children to walk ahead. Then Maria poured out the story of her lonely four years.

The University of Chicago had managed the Chicago part of the bomb development project. After the war it set up the Institute for Nuclear Studies (later the Enrico Fermi Institute). Scientists who had worked on the bomb, such as Enrico Fermi and Edward Teller, could stay together there and carry their studies of the atom in peaceful directions. The university also offered positions to scientists working in related areas, including Joe Mayer. It promised Maria Mayer a position as associate professor. She felt that Chicago was "the first place where I was not considered a nuisance, but greeted with open arms." Once again, however, anti-nepotism rules kept her from being paid. The Mayers moved to Chicago in February 1946.

The Chicago scientists got together at informal weekly seminars. Joe Mayer was the seminar leader. His only rule was, "Don't interrupt while someone else is interrupting." An observer at one of the seminars said it was "like sitting in on a conversation of the angels." These conversations inspired many visiting students, including the two young men whose ideas Chien-shiung Wu's experiments later would verify.

The scientists felt they were embarking on a new adventure together. They had learned how to split the atomic nucleus, but they knew very little about what the inside of the nucleus was like. They realized that its protons and neutrons were held together by powerful forces, but they did not know what those forces were. To study the nucleus the university built a giant cyclotron, in which atoms could be smashed apart with high-energy particles in a controlled way.

The U.S. government also set up the Argonne National Laboratory, which the University of Chicago would manage, to develop nuclear energy further. Robert G. Sachs became director of the Theory Division of the Argonne laboratory. He had been Maria Mayer's first graduate student. Sachs jumped at the chance to hire Mayer as a senior physicist on a half-time basis.

In 1947 Edward Teller asked Mayer to work with him on a theory about the origin of the chemical elements. In the process of doing this work, Mayer noticed that certain elements, such as lead and tin, were much more abundant than others. This had to mean that their nuclei were very stable. They did not break down or decay, thus turning into other elements, as (for example) uranium did.

Mayer found that most of these especially stable elements had either 50 or 82 neutrons or protons in their nuclei. She pointed out these special numbers to Teller and others. They came to be called her "magic numbers."

The list of magic numbers eventually grew to seven: 2, 8, 20, 28, 50, 82, and 126. Mayer collected data on many different elements from the scientists who were trying to break up the elements in the cyclotron and the nuclear reactor. She found that any element with a magic number's worth of either protons or neutrons was very stable. She published a paper on the magic numbers in April 1948.

Whether at work or at home, Mayer thought constantly about the numbers. "I kept thinking why, why, *why* do they exist?" she said later. "I thought the secret must be something we didn't know about how the nucleus of the atom is put together." She was right.

Mayer remembered that "magic" numbers of electrons also helped to make certain elements stable. Atoms with those numbers of electrons had an outer orbit or shell that was completely filled. No more electrons could be added without using a lot of energy.

Mayer wondered if the atom's nucleus also might be arranged in shells, like the layers of an onion. (When she began to describe her ideas to other physicists, one nicknamed her "the Madonna of the Onion.") If the magic numbers represented filled shells in the nucleus, they might keep elements from breaking down radioactively, just as filled electron shells kept atoms from reacting chemically. When elements break down radioactively, they turn into other elements by giving off nuclear particles.

Other scientists had suggested a shell model of the nucleus and had seen their ideas rejected. The most popular image of the nucleus in the late 1940s was one contributed by Niels Bohr. Bohr said the nucleus was like a drop of water. The protons and neutrons were held together tightly, Bohr believed, but they did not occupy particular places. Mayer was unaware that most physicists accepted the Bohr model.

Mayer believed that her "onion" idea solved part of the nuclear puzzle—but she knew that something was still missing. The last puzzle piece came to her one day in 1948 when she was talking to Enrico Fermi in her office. (Since her Columbia days Mayer had talked to Fermi about her ideas.) Someone stuck a head in the door and announced that Fermi had a phone call in his office. As Fermi walked out, he asked Mayer, "Is there any indication of spin-orbit coupling?"

Mayer suddenly realized that this was the answer to the mystery. "I got so excited it wiped everything out," she said later. She hardly saw Fermi leave; she was too busy with pencil and paper, working out a mathematical explanation of her ideas. She finished the basic calculations in 10 minutes.

When Fermi returned from his call, Mayer tried to tell him all about her insight with the rapid-fire speech she used when she was excited. Fermi, who preferred more methodical descriptions, smilingly stopped her. "Tomorrow, when you are less excited, you can explain it to me," he said.

Spin-orbit coupling refers to the fact that the direction in which a particle is spinning helps to determine which of two orbits it will occupy. All the particles in an orbit tend to spin in the same direction.

For electrons, the effect of spinning on a determined orbit—that is, of spin-orbit coupling—is very slight. This is because the energy needed for an electron to spin in one direction is about the same as the energy needed for it to spin the other way. Physicists had assumed that this was the case in the nucleus, too. Mayer, however, began calculating what would happen if the amounts of energy needed for nuclear particles to turn in different directions were very different. If this were the case, the effect of spin on orbit would be very strong. As Mayer later said to Marianne, when explaining the nucleus as a room full of dancers, "Everybody who has ever danced the fast waltz knows that it's easier to dance one way around than the other."

Mayer's calculations fit exactly what had been observed. Over and over her magic numbers appeared. As with electrons, Mayer concluded, they must be the numbers that meant shells were filled with particles or "closed."

At the end of the day, her calculations complete, Maria Mayer "floated home." As always, she told Joe everything. "You must publish immediately," he said.

Mayer was not sure she wanted to do so. As with her Ph.D. thesis long ago, Joe had to badger Maria into writing a full account. It finally appeared in the journal *Physical Review* in April 1950.

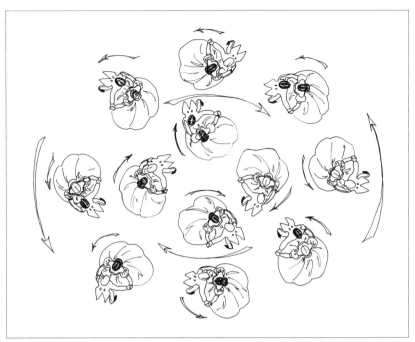

Shell theory and spin-orbit coupling. Maria Mayer explained to her daughter that particles in an atom's nucleus are like a roomful of waltzers. All the couples in each circle spin in the same direction. The whole circle also turns.
(Courtesy Katherine MacFarlane)

Joe Mayer was right to push his wife. If Maria had waited much longer, she admitted later, her idea would have resulted only in "experience" instead of in the Nobel Prize. She soon learned that a German scientist, Hans Jensen, had worked out the same theory at the same time.

Many scientists would have fought bitterly over who deserved the credit of being "first," but Maria Mayer was not that kind of person. Luckily, Hans Jensen wasn't either. Mayer and Jensen soon began exchanging friendly letters. In 1950 the two met in Germany. They agreed to collaborate on a book about "their" shell theory. *Elementary Theory of Nuclear Shell Structure* was published in 1955.

In 1959 the University of California asked both of the Mayers to be full—and fully paid—professors at its new San Diego campus.

Maria Goeppert Mayer

The Mayers moved to southern California in 1960 and bought a house by the sea. Unfortunately, Maria Mayer had a stroke only a few months after the move. It paralyzed her left arm and hand and weakened her right one. Nonetheless, she continued to work.

On November 5, 1963, when Maria Mayer was 57 years old, the Mayers' phone rang at four in the morning. It was a call from Stockholm, Sweden. Mayer had won the Nobel Prize, the world's most respected science prize, in physics!

Once the news sank in, Maria Mayer's response was, "Oh, good! I've always wanted to meet a king." She knew that King Gustav VI Adolf of Sweden would present the prize. On December 10, 1963, Mayer received her gold medal. She was only the second woman in the Nobel's history (Marie Curie was the first, in 1903) to win the prize in physics. She was the first American woman to win. She shared the prize with Jensen and Eugene Wigner, another nuclear physicist. Joe Mayer watched the ceremony with tears running down his face.

After a thrilling but exhausting week of celebrations, the Mayers returned to California. Life went back to normal. Maria continued her research and teaching. She refined her shell theory. She added to her list of honors, which (in addition to the Nobel Prize) included membership in the National Academy of Sciences and a collection of honorary doctorates. Maria Mayer died of heart disease on February 20, 1972, at the age of 65.

For Maria Goeppert Mayer, winning the Nobel Prize was a dream come true. Yet it was also something of an anticlimax. "Winning the prize wasn't half as exciting as doing the work itself," she told an interviewer several years later. "*That* was the fun—seeing it work out!"

Chronology

June 28, 1906	Maria Goeppert born in Kattowitz, Germany
1910	Goeppert family moves to Göttingen
1914	World War I begins
1924	Maria Goeppert enters Göttingen University
1930	marries Joseph Mayer; gets Ph.D. degree; moves to United States (Johns Hopkins)
1933	becomes U.S. citizen; Adolf Hitler takes power in Germany
1938	Mayers move to Columbia University
1939	first atomic fission experiments succeed; World War II begins in Europe
1941	Manhattan Project begins; United States enters World War II
1942	Mayer begins work on SAM project
1945	bombs dropped on Hiroshima and Nagasaki; World War II ends
1946	Mayers take jobs at University of Chicago
1947–49	Mayer's discovery of "magic numbers" leads to invention of shell theory of atomic nucleus
1959	Mayers take jobs at University of California, San Diego
December 10, 1963	Mayer receives Nobel Prize in physics
February 20, 1972	Maria Mayer dies

Further Reading

Dash, Joan. *A Life of One's Own*. New York: Harper & Row, 1973. Most detailed description of Maria Mayer's life; one-third of the book is devoted to her. Concentrates on her personal life.

_____. *The Triumph of Discovery*. Englewood Cliffs, N.J.: Julian Messner, 1991. Book for young adults on women who won the Nobel Prize. Devotes a chapter to Mayer.

Haber, Louis. *Women Pioneers of Science*. New York: Harcourt Brace Jovanovich, 1979. For young adults. Includes a chapter on Mayer.

Hall, Mary H. "Maria Mayer: The Marie Curie of the Atom." *McCall's*, July 1964. Focuses on Mayer's personal life; includes good quotes from her and others.

"Mayer, Maria Goeppert." *Current Biography*, 1964. Concise description of Mayer's life, written soon after she won the Nobel Prize.

Mayer, Maria Goeppert. "The Structure of the Nucleus." *Scientific American*, March 1951. Explains earlier discoveries about the atom as well as Mayer's shell theory. Difficult reading.

Opfell, Olga S. *The Lady Laureates*. Metuchen, N.J.: The Scarecrow Press, Inc., 1986. Includes a chapter on Mayer.

Sachs, Robert G. "Maria Goeppert Mayer: Two-fold Pioneer." *Physics Today*, February 1982. Written by Mayer's first graduate student and director of the Theory Division of the Argonne National Laboratory during Mayer's work there. Concentrates on Mayer's scientific career.

Shiels, Barbara. *Winners: Women and the Nobel Prize*. Minneapolis, Minn.: Dillon Press, 1985. For young adults. Includes a chapter on Mayer.

Grace Murray Hopper
(1906–1992)

*Grace Murray Hopper. Hopper made computers easier to use.
She said her greatest honor was serving "very proudly" in
the United States Navy, in which she became the
only woman admiral.*
(Courtesy Unisys Corporation)

Do you own a computer or know someone who does? If the computer is a laptop, it may not be much larger than this book. Today's computers are easy to use. Most people use commercial programs such as word processors or spreadsheets for financial calculations. They give orders to the machine by typing in simple commands or marking choices on a "menu."

The computer that Grace Murray Hopper faced when she reported for work on a navy project in July 1944 was very different. It was called the Mark I. It filled a large room in Harvard University's Cruft Laboratory. It weighed 5 tons and was 51 feet long and 8 feet high.

Hopper had to write a complicated program, or set of instructions, for each task she wanted the computer to do. Writing a program used all her ingenuity and mathematics training and could take days or weeks.

Grace Hopper played a large part in the changes that occurred between the Mark I and today's computers. She was the first to make a computer do part of its own programming. She helped to write the first computer programming language that used English words. Perhaps most important, she helped people understand how computers could help them and taught them how to use computers effectively.

Grace Brewster Murray was born on December 9, 1906, in New York City. She was the first child of Walter and Mary Murray. Her father was an insurance broker. Her great-grandfather on her mother's side had been a rear admiral in the navy during the Civil War. Grace remembered him as "tall and straight, carrying a black cane with a silver top on it."

Grace had fond memories of her grandfather on her mother's side, too. He was a senior civil engineer for the city of New York. As a child, she shared some of his engineering interests. One day she took apart all seven alarm clocks in her family's summer home. Unfortunately, she could not put any of them back together.

While Grace and her younger sister and brother were still children, their father became ill. Both of his legs had to be amputated. After that he walked on heavy wooden legs, using two canes. He did not let that stop him from working or leading a full life. He told his children that if he could get around on two wooden legs, *they* could do anything.

Grace Murray entered Vassar, a women's college in Poughkeepsie, New York, in 1924. She majored in mathematics and physics. She graduated in 1928 and then went on to Yale University. She received a master's degree in mathematics from Yale in 1930.

27

On June 15 of that same year, Grace Murray married Vincent Foster Hopper. Hopper was a teacher of English and literature. Grace Hopper continued her graduate work after her marriage, getting her Ph.D. from Yale in 1934. She also began teaching mathematics at Vassar in 1931.

After the United States entered World War II, Grace Hopper decided to join the navy. She and her husband had separated by then; they were divorced in 1945. She was sworn into the United States Naval Reserve in December 1943.

After two months of military training, Hopper was assigned to work on the Bureau of Ordnance (gunnery) Computation Project at Harvard University. (Maria Mayer and Chien-shiung Wu were doing war work on the atomic bomb project at this time.) That was when Hopper met the Mark I, one of the first modern computers. Howard Aiken, a Harvard mathematics professor, had designed the immense machine.

Aiken, who was also a commander in the Naval Reserve, was waiting when Hopper arrived at Harvard's Cruft Laboratory on July 2, 1944. "That's a computing engine," he told her, pointing at the Mark I. "I would be delighted to have the coefficients for the interpolation of the arc tangent by next Thursday."

Hopper admitted later that she was "scared to death" by the hulking machine. But she said she also thought, "Gee, that's the prettiest gadget I ever saw."

The Mark I was powered by electricity, but thousands of mechanical switches or relays opened and closed during its operation. The relays told the computer what numbers to work with. When the computer was calculating, Hopper said, the clacking

The Mark I computer. This "granddaddy" of modern computers was 51 feet long and 8 feet high. Grace Hopper was one of its first programmers.
(Courtesy Cruft Photo Lab, Harvard University)

sound of the moving relays sounded like a roomful of people knitting.

Instructions to the computer were coded as holes punched into paper tape. They told the machine what calculations to perform and in what order. The computer carried out the instructions by turning sets of relays on or off. It printed the results on electric typewriters attached to the machine.

The Mark I could carry out three additions every second. That is unbelievably slow compared to today's computers, but then it seemed like a miracle. In one day the machine could do calculations that would have taken a person six months.

The Mark I's first job was to perform the complex calculations needed to aim new navy guns accurately. Later it also did calculations for self-propelled rockets and new kinds of mines. The navy needed this information quickly, so the Mark I ran 24 hours a day. So did the crew of eight who programmed it, Grace Hopper included. They often slept on their desks so they could leap into action immediately if the computer developed a problem.

Hopper encountered her most famous computer failure in the summer of 1945. At that time the Mark II, the Mark I's successor, was being built in the Harvard lab. When the new machine suddenly stopped working, Hopper and the rest of the crew looked for the problem. Finally they found the body of a two-inch moth jammed into a failed relay. The moth apparently had flown into the relay and was beaten to death. The crew extracted the insect with tweezers and taped it into the logbook that Commander Aiken demanded they keep. After that, whenever Aiken demanded to know why the crew was not "making any numbers," they would say, "We're debugging the computer." *Debugging* is still the term computer people use for "trying to find and fix problems."

In the 1940s, when the cumbersome Harvard computers were almost the only ones in existence, most people thought that computer use would never become widespread. The machines seemed too big, too hard to use, and too expensive to appeal to businesspeople. J. Prosper Eckert and John Mauchly were among the few who believed otherwise. While Hopper and her cohorts were debugging the early Marks, Eckert and Mauchly built the world's first general-purpose electronic computer at the University of Pennsylvania. It was called ENIAC, which was short for Electronic Numerical Integrator And Calculator.

ENIAC dwarfed even the Mark I. It was over 100 feet long and 10 feet high, and it weighed more than 30 tons. Instead of mechanical relays it used over 18,000 glass vacuum tubes. It needed so much electricity that people claimed all the lights in Philadelphia dimmed when it was turned on.

Eckert and Mauchly formed a business to make computers in 1946. Grace Hopper met them when they asked her to write a program for the Prudential Insurance Company. She came to share their interest in adapting computers for business use. She joined their company in 1949. By then they were working on ENIAC's successor, EDVAC (Electronic Discrete Variable Automatic Computer), which was finished in 1952.

EDVAC made two advances that became standard in later computers. First, it had a much larger memory than ENIAC. Among other things, this meant that both the numbers needed for a computation and the instructions for the calculation could be stored in the computer's memory. Working with data and instructions saved in memory is much faster than having to enter everything into the computer for each job. EDVAC's second advance was displaying numbers in a binary number system instead of converting them to the more familiar decimal number system. The binary system uses only 1, which stands for "on," and 0, which stands for "off." Using the binary system meant that EDVAC needed far fewer vacuum tubes and thus less electricity than ENIAC. The lights of Philadelphia presumably could go back to normal operation.

In 1951 Eckert and Mauchly built the first mass-produced commercial computer, UNIVAC (Universal Automatic Computer) I. UNIVAC I had several kinds of memory and used high-speed magnetic tape instead of paper tape or punched cards to record data. It was also smaller than the earlier computers, being a mere 14 ½ feet long and 7 ½ feet high. It was 1,000 times faster than the Mark I.

Now that computers were becoming more powerful, Grace Hopper realized they could be made to write parts of their own programs. "Nobody believed it could be done," Hopper told an interviewer later. "Yet it was so obvious. Why start from scratch with every single program you write? Develop one that would do a lot of the basic work over and over again."

Hopper designed a new kind of computer program called a compiler. She put a variety of programming routines into the computer on magnetic tape and gave each routine a "call number." Then she put in another program that used the call numbers in mathematical equations. Using the compiler program, the computer found the routines and put them together in the order specified by the call numbers. With a compiler, programmers could prepare in five minutes a program that formerly would have taken a month to write. Compilers also made programming more accurate because they prevented the mistakes that occurred when people typed in the same programming routines over and over.

By the middle of 1952, when she wrote her first compiler, Grace Hopper was able to brag, "I could make a computer do anything which I could completely define." At that time she was working for Remington Rand, which had bought the Eckert-Mauchly Corporation in 1950. (Remington Rand later merged into the Sperry Corporation, which later became Unisys.) Pleased with Hopper's compiler, Remington Rand gave her the post of systems engineer, director of automatic programming development.

A few large businesses and scientific research institutions bought computers in the early 1950s. Most businesses, however, wanted nothing to do with the machines. Computers were still bulky, expensive, and, above all, difficult to use. Even with compilers, programmers had to learn what amounted to a foreign language.

Grace Hopper decided there was no reason why computer programs could not be written in English. The first compilers had used mathematical symbols, but letters of the alphabet were also symbols. They could be used just as well. "No one thought of that earlier," she said, "because they weren't as lazy as I was. A lot of our programmers like to play with the bits. I wanted to get jobs done. That's what the computer was there for."

Hopper recognized that businesses also needed to get jobs done. If computers could be programmed in a familiar language, businesspeople might be more willing to use them. Using words in programming also would be helpful because business information is not all mathematical. A program that keeps track of a company's payroll, for example, must include both numbers and words, such as employees' names.

In 1957 Hopper began work on a computer language called Flowmatic. Even more than a compiler, the language let programmers write in terms that humans could understand. It then translated these terms into a form that computers could understand. Flowmatic was the first computer language to use English words for both the data to be operated on and the instructions for the operations.

Other companies soon developed computer languages, too. Different computers used different languages. Hopper and others realized that the industry needed a standard language that could be used on any computer. That would allow programmers working for different companies, using different machines, to share each other's work.

Representatives of several major computer companies met on April 8, 1959. They agreed to develop a universal programming language for business. After about a year of work, Hopper and a committee of other programmers prepared a language called COBOL (COmmon Business Oriented Language). Hopper has been called "the mother of COBOL" because her Flowmatic language was COBOL's direct ancestor.

COBOL is still the computer language most widely used in business. For one thing, it is fairly easy for people who are not computer experts to understand. (Like all computer languages, however, COBOL follows strict rules that are not always the same as the rules for English. Only certain English words can be used in COBOL programs, for example.) COBOL also works well for handling large amounts of the kinds of information that businesses use.

During all the years she worked for business, Grace Hopper remained a consultant for the Naval Reserve. In 1966, however, a letter from the Reserve's Chief of Personnel ordered her to apply for retirement. She was then 60 years old and had been on reserve duty for over 20 years. Hopper reluctantly complied. She was placed on the retired list with the rank of commander at the end of the year. "It was the saddest day of my life," Hopper said later.

It proved to be a very short retirement—seven months, to be exact. The government wanted to use COBOL, but different companies had developed different versions of the language. Some versions did not work on some computers. Norman Ream, former special assistant to the secretary of the navy, asked Grace Hopper to standardize COBOL for the navy.

"I came running—I always do when the Navy sends for me," Hopper said. She returned to temporary active duty on August 1, 1967. This "temporary" duty was to last another 19 years. Hopper once remarked that it was "the longest six months I've ever spent."

Hopper and her staff set up standards for COBOL that allowed the language to be used on most computers. They developed "certifier" programs that told users whether a compiler that claimed to use COBOL met those standards. They also wrote

```
PROCEDURE DIVISION
PRINT-REPORT SECTION.
  •
  •

    PERFORM PRINT-ELEMENT THRU PRINT-ELEMENT-EXIT
        UNTIL REG-END-OF-FILE.
    COMPUTE AVERAGE-FEE = TOTAL-FEES-PAID /
TOTAL-REG-COUNT.
  •
  •

PRINT-ELEMENT.
**
**  READ AND PRINT A SINGLE RECORD.
**  ACCUMULATE STATISTICS.
**

    READ REG-RECORD INTO REG-WORK-RECORD
        AT END MOVE 'E' TO REG-FLAG-ST
            GO TO PRINT-ELEMENT-EXIT.

    ADD 1 TO TOTAL-REG-RECORDS.
    IF REG-WORK-DONT-MAIL
        ADD 1 TO UNMAILABLE-RECORDS
        GO TO PRINT-ELEMENT-EXIT.

    MOVE SPACES TO PRINT-LINE-1.
    MOVE '0' TO PL1-CARRIAGE-CONTROL.
    ADD 2 TO LINE-COUNT.

    MOVE REG-WORK-LAST-NAME PL1-LAST-NAME.
  •
  •
  •

    WRITE PRINT-FILE FROM PRINT-LINE-1.
    IF LINE-COUNT GREATER THAN PAGE-LENGTH
        PERFORM PAGE-HEADER THROUGH PAGE-HEADER-EXIT.

PRINT-ELEMENT-EXIT.
    EXIT.
```

Sample of COBOL code. Grace Hopper helped to develop COBOL, the first widely used programming language to contain English words. COBOL is still the programming language that large businesses use most.
(Courtesy Hal Heydt)

manuals that taught COBOL programming. Hopper traveled around the country showing people how to use computers and COBOL.

Ream also gave Hopper a second task: persuading the entire navy to use COBOL in its computing. This was much harder than standardizing the language. Over and over, navy bureaucrats resisted her suggestions by saying, "But we've always done it this way!" Hopper used to threaten, "I'm going to shoot somebody for saying that someday." Using humor and persuasion, she eventually brought most of the resisters around. "Grace Hopper was the best public relations person the Navy ever had," Rear Admiral Peter Cullins has said. In sharing her enthusiasm and helping ordinary people understand a technical subject, Grace Hopper did for computers what Eugenie Clark did for undersea life and Candace Pert did for brain chemistry.

Grace Hopper retired from the Sperry Corporation in 1971. She continued her work for the navy, however. She was promoted to the rank of captain in 1973. She also became a visiting professor or lecturer at several colleges. She always gave her students two pieces of advice. One was to try new ideas whether others approve of them or not, "because it is much easier to apologize later than it is to get permission." The other was, "A ship in port is safe, but that is not what ships are for. Be good ships: sail out to sea and do new things." Hopper claimed that the young people she taught were her greatest achievement.

Hopper predicted in the early 1970s that computers would become "the largest industry in the United States." In the next two decades she saw her words come true. Computers became smaller and cheaper. By the 1980s, not only small businesses but many individuals could afford the machines. Computers millions of times more powerful than the venerable Mark I now can be bought for about a thousand dollars.

In her later years, Grace Hopper turned her attention away from the technical details of programming. Instead, she spoke about the way people and companies use information. People waste time and money in computing, she said, because they do not think about how they use information and which information is important to them. They need to plan programs that give the most attention to the most important information. They also need to make sure that their information is accurate, complete, and tells them what they really need to know.

Grace Hopper received many awards during her long career. The first was the Naval Ordance Development Award, which was presented to her in 1946. In 1973 she received the Legion of Merit, an award given to United States military personnel for performance of outstanding services. In 1983 the navy promoted her to the rank of commodore. She was inducted into the Engineering and Science Hall of Fame in 1984. Several facilities were named after her, including the navy's Grace Murray Hopper Service Center in San Diego, California. Hopper won the National Medal of Technology in 1991.

Perhaps the award that pleased Grace Hopper most was the one she received on November 8, 1985. On that day the navy raised her rank to rear admiral, making her the only woman admiral in the history of the United States. She warned her friends in Philadelphia to keep an eye on her great-grandfather's grave because he might "rise from the dead" at the idea of a woman admiral!

When asked what she found to be the greatest reward of her career, however, Grace Hopper always gave the same answer. It was "the privilege and responsibility of serving with true faith and allegiance, very proudly, in the United States Navy."

Grace Hopper finally retired from the navy for good on August 14, 1986, at the age of 79. She was by then the oldest commissioned officer on active duty in the United States Navy. At her request, her retirement ceremonies were held aboard the *U.S.S. Constitution*, the country's oldest commissioned warship. During the ceremonies Admiral Hopper was given the Distinguished Service Medal, the Department of Defense's highest honor, and a long-stemmed rose for each of the 43 years of her career.

Even that did not mark the end of Grace Hopper's working life. After leaving the navy, she became a consultant for Digital Equipment Corporation. "I seem to do an awful lot of retiring, but I don't think I will ever be able to really retire," she said.

The *Constitution* has the nickname of "Old Ironsides." Grace Hopper gained nicknames during her career, too. She was sometimes called "Grandma COBOL" or "The Grand Old Lady of Software." (*Software* is another term for computer programs.) Most commonly and lovingly, however, she was known as "Amazing Grace." She died at age 85 on January 1, 1992.

Chronology

December 9, 1906	Grace Brewster Murray born
1928	earns B.A. in mathematics and physics from Vassar
1930	earns master's degree in mathematics from Yale; marries Vincent Hopper
1934	earns Ph.D. from Yale
December 1943	joins WAVES (Naval Reserve)
July 2, 1944	reports for duty at Ordnance Computation Project and sees Mark I for first time
1945	divorced from Vincent Hopper
1949	joins Eckert-Mauchly Corporation
1951	UNIVAC, first commercial computer, built
1952	Hopper designs first compiler
1957	develops Flowmatic computer language
1959–60	helps develop COBOL
1966	retires from navy
1967	called back to active duty
1971	retires from Sperry Corporation
1984	inducted into Engineering and Science Hall of Fame
November 8, 1985	promoted to rear admiral
August 14, 1986	retires from navy
January 1, 1992	Hopper dies

Further Reading

Augarten, Stan. *Bit by Bit.* New York: Ticknor and Fields, 1984. Provides background on the history of computers, up to the beginning of the personal computer era (1980s).

Barron, Janet J., ed. "Prioritizing Information." *Byte,* May 1991. In remarks from a speech and interview, Grace Hopper explains how businesses should handle information.

Billings, Charlene W. *Grace Hopper.* Hillside, N.J.: Enslow Publishers, 1989. For young adults. Book-length biography of Hopper, full of interesting quotes.

"The Grand Old Lady of Software." *Newsweek,* May 9, 1983. Short article describes Hopper's contributions to the computer industry.

Levitas, Louise. "She Tamed the Thinking Machine." *Science Digest,* March 1956. Written soon after Hopper invented compilers, this article reviews her achievements up to that point.

Rausa, Captain Rosario M. "Grace Murray Hopper." *Naval History,* Fall 1992. Article written after Hopper's death provides a detailed review of her career.

Slater, Robert. *Portraits in Silicon.* Cambridge: Massachusetts Institute of Technology Press, 1987. Book on important people in computer history devotes a chapter to Hopper.

Chien-shiung Wu
(1912–)

Chien-shiung Wu. Wu studied the inside of the atom and performed experiments that disproved a basic law of physics.
(Courtesy AIP Emilio Segrè Visual Archives)

*L*ook in a mirror, and your twin looks back at you. Wave at your twin, and your twin waves back. But if you wave with your right hand, is your twin doing the same—or is the twin waving with the left hand?

As Maria Mayer noticed, particles in the nucleus of atoms also have mirror-image twins. The twins differ in the direction that the particles spin; one spins clockwise, the other spins counterclockwise. They could be called right-handed or left-handed, just as people speak of right-handed or left-handed screws.

In identifying spin-orbit coupling, Mayer pointed out one difference in the way the "twins" can behave. Since 1925, however, physicists had believed that in general, the laws of physics made no distinction between objects (including subatomic particles) and their mirror images. This belief was called the law of conservation of parity (parity means equality or equivalence). The law of parity, as it was called for short, was regarded as a fundamental law of nature. Nuclear physicists built many other theories on it.

In 1957 the careful measurements of a Chinese-born woman physicist changed all that. Following up the ideas of two other Chinese-American physicists, Chien-shiung (pronounced Chen-shung) Wu proved that the law of parity did not always hold. In doing so, like Maria Mayer, she changed the way scientists viewed the world of the atom. A reporter called her achievement "the most important development in nuclear physics since the . . . unleashing of atomic energy."

Chien-shiung Wu was born in Liu-ho, a town near Shanghai, China, on May 29, 1912. Her father, Wu Zong-yee (Chinese place their family names first), was a school principal. He believed that women had as much right to a good education as men. He encouraged his daughter as well as his two sons to read the many books in his library and to plan for college and a professional career. Chien-shiung Wu said later that her father was "always ahead of his time." However, she has also pointed out that "there was nothing unusual about women students in China."

Chien-shiung went to high school in Soochow. There she studied English, mathematics, and other subjects. She discovered that physics was her favorite. "Somehow I soon knew it was what I wanted to go on with." She continued her math and physics studies at the National Central University in Nanking, from which she got her bachelor's degree in 1936.

By then war was looming over China. There were clashes with Japan, and within the country Nationalist and Communist factions were fighting. Partly because of this threat and partly because she wanted the best education possible, Chien-shiung decided to do her graduate work in the United States.

Chien-shiung Wu chose the University of California at Berkeley for her graduate studies. It was a wise choice. Berkeley in the late 1930s was as exciting a place for a young nuclear physicist as Maria Mayer's Göttingen had been in the late 1920s. Ernest O. Lawrence, who had just been put in charge of the university's radiation laboratory, was building the first cyclotron, or "atom smasher." In this machine, high-energy particles crashed into and shattered atomic nuclei. By studying the particles that emerged, nuclear physicists learned that the inside of the atom was much more complex than anyone had dreamed.

As a graduate student, Chien-shiung Wu impressed Lawrence and her other professors with two skills that would make her famous all her life. One was her ability to design an experiment that could prove or disprove a theory. The other was her care in making extremely accurate measurements. It was later said that "she has virtually never made a mistake in her measurements." In these talents she was very different from Maria Mayer. Mayer's work was in the realm of theories and ideas, whereas Wu was an experimental physicist.

Wu did her graduate research on beta decay, a form of radioactive breakdown in which an atomic nucleus gives off a high-energy particle. She studied beta decay during most of her career. Wu got her Ph.D. from Berkeley in 1940.

In 1942 Wu married Luke Chia-liu Yuan, who had been a fellow physics student at Berkeley. Wu continued to use her maiden name professionally. Wu and Yuan had a son, Vincent, in 1945.

After Wu's marriage, she taught physics for a year at Smith College in Northampton, Massachusetts. She then became the first woman to teach at Princeton, then an all-male university in New Jersey. She had been there only a few months, however, when the U.S. government asked her to work on the top-secret Manhattan Project, which resulted in the atomic bomb. In March 1944 she went to Columbia University in New York and joined the Division of War Research. Like Maria Mayer, she tried to find ways to increase the amount of fissionable uranium that could be made available for the bomb. (The two did not work together, but they may have met.) Wu also helped to improve Geiger counters, which detect radiation.

After the war Wu became a research associate at Columbia, where she was to spend the rest of her career. In 1952 she became an associate professor. She became a naturalized citizen of the United States in 1954. Wu continued her work on beta decay, designing experiments to test other physicists' theories about the process.

Meanwhile, Tsung Dao Lee and Chen Ning Yang, two young Chinese-American men, were beginning to question what had been thought of as a basic law of physics. As graduate students, they had sat in on some of the "conversations of the angels" held by Enrico Fermi, Maria Mayer, and others at the University of Chicago. By the mid-1950s Lee, like Wu, was at Columbia, while Yang was at the Institute for Advanced Studies at Princeton.

Lee and Yang became intrigued by what nuclear physicists called the "tau-theta puzzle." Scientists had discovered in 1952 that when certain atomic nuclei were broken apart, short-lived particles called K-mesons flew out. Two kinds of K-mesons, called tau and theta, had the same mass. According to the law of parity, they should have broken down in the same way—but they did not. The tau K-meson broke down into three particles called pi mesons, whereas the theta K-meson decayed into two pi mesons.

Most physicists assumed that this apparent difference in behavior was due to some kind of experimental error. Lee and Yang, however, boldly suggested that the law of parity itself might not be valid, at least for the so-called weak nuclear interactions that were involved in radioactive decay. They described their ideas in a scientific paper in 1956.

Lee and Yang looked for experimental nuclear physicists to test their ideas. One name that came first to their minds was Chien-shiung Wu. They suggested an experiment that Wu could do, but Wu herself had to find a way to carry out the work. The experiment used cobalt-60, a radioactive form of the element cobalt. If cobalt-60 was placed in a strong electromagnetic field, the field would make all the cobalt nuclei line up like little magnets. Then they would all spin along the same axis. At room temperature, however, heat energy made the nuclei move around so much that this effect was destroyed. To make the experiment succeed, Wu would have to perform it at unbelievably low temperatures.

Wu joined forces with a research team at the National Bureau of Standards in Washington, D.C. The bureau had one of the few laboratories in the country that could chill material to extremely low temperatures. Using the bureau's apparatus, Wu cooled cobalt-60 to .01 degree above absolute zero (−273.15° Celsius or −459.67° Fahrenheit). Absolute zero is the temperature at which all atomic motion due to heat is stopped. Radioactive decay, however, is not affected. At this low temperature, the effect of the magnet on the cobalt nuclei was strong.

Now Wu measured exactly what happened when the cobalt nuclei broke down. Using a device called a scintillation counter, she determined how many particles shot out in the direction of the magnetic field's spin. She compared this number to the number of particles that flew in the opposite direction. If the law of parity was correct, the nuclei should give off equal numbers of particles in both directions. If Lee and Yang were right, however, more particles should be given off in one direction than in the other.

Wu did the experiment over and over to make sure her counts were accurate. During the final days of testing she averaged four hours of sleep a night. "It was like a nightmare," she said after it was all over. "I wouldn't want to go through [it] again."

In the end, however, the results of the experiment were clear. Wu found that far more particles flew off in the direction opposite the nuclei's spin than in the direction that matched the spin. This proved that the beta decay of cobalt-60 behaved like a left-handed screw. It also proved that Lee and Yang were right: the law of parity did not hold for weak nuclear interactions.

Wu announced her results on January 16, 1957. She caused a scientific sensation. A reporter in the New York *Post* wrote that "this small, modest woman was powerful enough to do what armies can never accomplish: she helped destroy a law of nature." Her findings were soon confirmed by other experiments at Columbia and at the University of Chicago.

Wu was excited by what her discovery might mean. "We have no idea now what [it] will lead to," she said. "The sudden liberation of our thinking on the very structure of the physical world has been overwhelming." She added, "In place of parity conservation there may be a deeper symmetry connecting, for the first time, space and electric charge."

Lee and Yang received the Nobel Prize in 1957 for their groundbreaking ideas. Although Wu did not share in that prize, she won a number of other awards during 1958. For example, she became the seventh woman elected to the National Academy of Sciences. She also became the first woman to receive an honorary doctorate from Princeton. In offering her the degree, the university's president said that Wu had "richly earned the right to be called the world's foremost female experimental physicist." Wu became a full professor at Columbia in 1958 as well.

After Wu's work in disproving the law of parity, Emilio Segrè, who had been one of her teachers at Berkeley, hailed her as "the reigning queen of nuclear physics." She was a queen to her students at Columbia as well. She had a modest but dignified air that went well with her traditional side-slitted Chinese dress (the cheongsam) and the hair she bound neatly back in a bun. However, some observers called her a "slave driver." If she was, she did not ask anything of her students that she did not also demand of

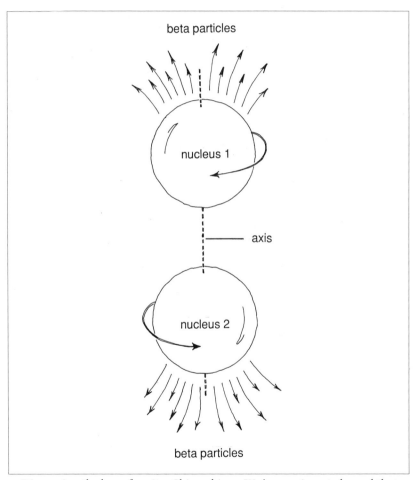

beta particles

nucleus 1

axis

nucleus 2

beta particles

Disproving the law of parity. Chien-shiung Wu's experiment showed that when cobalt-60 nuclei broke down, more particles flew out of the nuclei in one direction than in the other. This was not what the law of parity predicted. Nucleus 2 in the drawing is the mirror image of nucleus 1.
(Courtesy Katherine MacFarlane)

herself. She once said, "I have always felt that in physics, and probably in other endeavors, too, you must have total commitment. It is not just a job. It is a way of life."

Chien-shiung Wu carried out several other important experiments during her years at Columbia. In 1963, for example, she tested a theory about beta decay that had been proposed in 1958 by nuclear physicists Richard Feynman and Murray Gell-Mann. The theory stated that an energy called vector current is conserved during coupling and disintegration of subatomic particles. Wu showed that the decay of certain forms of boron and nitrogen occurred in a way that fitted predictions made by the conservation theory.

Wu carried out another experiment 2,000 feet (600 meters) underground in a salt mine near Cleveland, Ohio. She worked in a small house built to protect researchers from dangerous fumes that gathered in the mine. This experiment studied the beta decay of very long-lived calcium nuclei. The experiment could not be done at the surface of the earth because invisible rays from outer space, called cosmic rays, strike the earth all the time. These rays pass through living things harmlessly, but they would throw off the results of the delicate experiment. Because the earth absorbs cosmic rays, doing the experiment underground let Wu get accurate results.

Most of Wu's work seemed far removed from everyday life, but there was one exception. Columbia is located on the edge of Harlem, a part of New York City where many African-Americans live. Wu became aware of an inherited disease called sickle-cell anemia that affects mostly people of African descent. Hemoglobin, the substance in the blood that carries oxygen to body cells, is defective in this disease.

Iron is a vital part of the hemoglobin molecule. Chien-shiung Wu used her skill in experimental nuclear physics to try to find out how the iron atoms in sickle-cell hemoglobin differ from those in normal hemoglobin. Her work did not result in new treatments for the disease. Still, it did show that, as Wu said, "even the most sophisticated and seemingly remote basic nuclear physics research has implications beneficial to human welfare."

Wu continued to receive awards and honors for her work. In 1964, soon after she proved the vector current theory, she became the first woman to win the Comstock Award of the National Academy of Sciences. In 1974 *Industrial Research* magazine named her its scientist of the year. In 1975 Wu became the first woman president of the prestigious American Physical Society. President Gerald Ford presented Wu with the National Medal of Science, the country's highest science award, in 1976. She received Israel's Wolf Prize in 1978.

Wu retired from Columbia University in the late 1980s. She presently lives in New York City with her husband.

The importance of Chien-shiung Wu's work can perhaps best be summed up by two statements she made soon after the experiment that disproved the law of parity. She said that because of the new developments to which she had contributed, "Physicists are now viewing Nature with a new understanding. . . . When we arrive at this understanding, we shall marvel how neatly all the elementary particles fit into the great scheme." In an address to National Science Award students in 1958 she added, "Science is not static but ever-growing and dynamic. . . . It is the courage to doubt what has long been established, the incessant search for its verification and proof, that pushed the wheel of science forward." Wu has certainly done more than her share in advancing that wheel.

Chronology

May 29, 1912	Chien-shiung Wu born in Liu-ho, China
1936	gets bachelor's degree from National Central University in Nanking
1940	gets Ph.D. from University of California at Berkeley
1942	marries Luke Chia-liu Yuan
1944	joins Division of War Research at Columbia
1952	becomes associate professor of physics at Columbia
1954	becomes naturalized citizen of United States
1956	Tsung Dao Lee and Chen Ning Yang publish paper suggesting that law of parity does not hold for weak interactions in atomic nucleus
January 16, 1957	Wu announces result of experiment that proves Lee and Yang's ideas
1958	becomes full professor at Columbia; wins awards including honorary doctorate at Princeton
1963	does experiment that proves theory about conservation of vector current
1975	becomes first woman president of American Physical Society
1976	receives National Medal of Science
late 1980s	retires from Columbia University

Further Reading

"Death of a Law." *Time,* January 28, 1957. Describes Wu's work in disproving the law of parity.

Noble, Iris. *Contemporary Women Scientists of America.* New York: Julian Messner, 1979. For young adults. Chapter on Wu clearly describes her life and work.

"Nuclear Theory Verified." *Science News Letter,* February 9, 1964. Describes Wu's experiment to confirm theory about conservation of vector current; difficult reading.

"Queen of Physics." *Newsweek,* May 20, 1963. Describes Wu's personality and reviews her work.

"Wu, Chien-shiung." *Current Biography,* 1959. Review of Wu's life and early career, focusing on her work in disproving the law of parity.

"Wu, Chien-shiung." *McGraw-Hill Modern Scientists and Engineers.* McGraw-Hill, 1980. Biographical sketch and review of Wu's work; difficult reading.

Yost, Edna. *Women of Modern Science.* New York: Dodd, Mead, 1962. For young adults. Devotes a chapter to Wu.

Gertrude Belle Elion
(1918–)

*Gertrude Belle Elion. Elion developed drugs that saved the
lives of people with cancer, kidney trouble,
and other diseases.*
(Courtesy Burroughs Wellcome Co.)

*I*magine a party in a hospital. People from many different wards
are there. A little girl, temporarily bald because of the medicines
she has been taking, is recovering from cancer. A middle-aged
man has just received a new kidney, freeing him from twice-
weekly trips to a hospital machine that more or less did the work
of his own failed kidneys. A young woman wears a bandage over
one eye. She has narrowly escaped blindness caused by a virus
disease.

Gertrude Belle Elion

There is no question who this party's guest of honor should be. Her name is Gertrude Elion. Elion created drugs that have saved the lives and restored the health of many thousands of people like the guests at this imaginary party. Her work has also given scientists important information about the chemistry of the human body.

———

Gertrude Belle Elion was born on January 23, 1918. She grew up in the Bronx, a part of New York City. Her father was a dentist and hoped that she and her brother would be, too. But "neither one of us was keen on dentistry," she says.

A tragedy turned young Trudy Elion's interest to medical research. The summer she graduated from high school—at age 15—her grandfather died "horribly" of cancer. Out of Trudy's grief grew "the realization that maybe I could do something about it."

Trudy went to Hunter College, in New York City, where she studied chemistry. She graduated with the highest honors in 1937. Without a scholarship, however, she could not afford to go to graduate school—and scholarships were almost impossible for women to get.

So were jobs in those later years of the Great Depression. One laboratory head refused to hire Trudy Elion because, he said, she would be a "distracting influence" on the men in the lab. One other lab hired her but did not pay her a salary at first. Elion later found work as a food analyst, checking to make sure that a company's pickles were sour enough and that berries intended for jam were not moldy. She taught high school for a while, too. During that period she went to graduate classes at New York University at night and on weekends. Elion got her master's degree in chemistry in 1941.

Another tragedy struck Gertrude Elion's life at this time. She became engaged to a young man, but before they could marry, he became ill and died. "I just never found anyone that would take his place," Elion says. "And then, when I got so involved in my work, I didn't look anymore." Elion never married.

A larger tragedy, World War II, brought better luck to Elion and many other women. When young men left home to serve in the war, women stepped into their jobs. "It was probably the war that gave me the opportunity to get into research," Elion says.

Burroughs Wellcome, a New York drug company, hired Elion in 1944. She became a research assistant in the laboratory of

George Hitchings, an older scientist who had joined Wellcome two years earlier. Elion's main job was to study the chemistry of the compounds the lab was working on. However, she soon became involved in finding out how these compounds worked in living cells as well. "There was no hierarchy that said, 'Well, you're a chemist, you can't do this,'" she recalls. She says that Hitchings's encouragement and the freedom in his small lab "helped me spread my wings much faster than I might have done in a larger place."

Elion and Hitchings were studying nucleic acids. These complex chemicals are in the nucleus, or center part, of every cell in the body. They carry the information that each living thing inherits from its parents. The information is coded in the arrangement of the four kinds of small molecules called bases that are part of the large nucleic acid molecules. (In a somewhat similar way, the meaning of words is coded in the arrangement of the letters of the alphabet.) The information in nucleic acids tells the cell how to carry out its activities and make the other chemicals it needs.

When a cell divides, it makes a new copy of its nucleic acids. That way, each of the two new cells will have a copy. The cell assembles the copy from bases and other chemicals that it takes in from outside. Hitchings and Elion were looking for ways to make bases that were just a little different from the natural ones. These changed bases could not be used to make new nucleic acids. If cancer cells or harmful bacteria could be "fooled" into taking up these bases, they would be unable to divide, and they would soon die. Thus the changed bases could be used as drugs to destroy the harmful cells or bacteria. These changed compounds were called antimetabolites because they kept cells from carrying out normal metabolism, or chemical activities.

Modifying compounds and substituting them for natural substances in cells was a more rational way of designing drugs than the hit-and-miss procedures most companies used. The advantage of this approach was that different changes made to the same compound could produce different drugs. "You were essentially feeling your way by making the [chemical] group a little larger," Elion has said.

Elion saw the drugs she worked on as "not only ends in themselves but . . . as tools for unlocking doors and probing Nature's mysteries." For example, Elion might study the way a drug was broken down

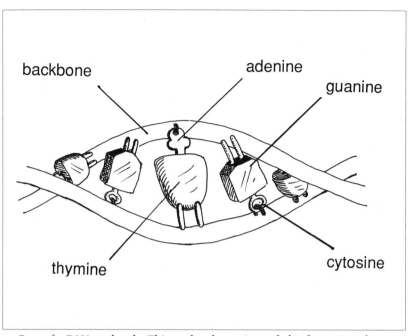

backbone

adenine

guanine

thymine

cytosine

Part of a DNA molecule. This molecule carries coded information that a living thing inherits from its parents. The four bases are the "letters" in the code. They always occur in pairs. They are attached to a "backbone" of sugar and phosphate. Gertrude Elion poisoned cancer cells by making them take up chemicals slightly different from the natural bases.
(Courtesy Katherine MacFarlane)

inside cells. She could find out whether, say, a cancer cell broke down the drug differently than a normal cell did. If it did, she would try to find out why. These chemical studies, in turn, often led to the discovery of new drugs. Thus Elion's basic and applied research constantly fed into each other.

Designing antimetabolite drugs systematically was a new idea. Only a few other scientists were doing it—and none of them was working on nucleic acids. At that time, little was known about the structure of these complex chemicals. "We knew something about the building blocks—the bits and pieces—but we didn't know how to put them together," Elion says. "People thought it was a little bit, not only brave but kind of stupid of us to think that we could get a . . . base that was abnormal into . . . nucleic acid, because no one had done that before."

Elion's work succeeded, however, and at last it gave her a chance to "do something about" cancer. In 1951 she developed a compound called 6-mercaptopurine. It was the first drug to fight cancer successfully by interfering with cancer cells' nucleic acid. The new drug proved especially helpful to children with leukemia, a cancer of certain cells in the blood. Before 6-mercaptopurine was used, most children with leukemia lived only a few months. 6-mercaptopurine helped them live longer—a year or more. It is still used, together with other drugs, to treat leukemia and certain other cancers. These drug combinations cure almost 80 percent of children with leukemia. Thus Gertrude Elion, like Helen Taussig, has helped to save sick children's lives, though Elion did not work directly with children as Taussig did. Like Candace Pert and Flossie Wong-Staal, Elion made her contribution to medicine through chemistry.

6-mercaptopurine was far from a perfect drug. Children given it often got better for a while, then became sick again and died. This high relapse rate "gave us a terrible sinking feeling," Elion says. She spent six more years tinkering with the compound, trying to find a way to make it more effective.

One relative of 6-mercaptopurine that Elion made was called azathioprine. This drug worked no better against cancer than its "parent," so Elion set it aside. But she did not forget it. "How you handle setbacks [in scientific research] can make a difference," Elion once told an interviewer. "You must never feel that you have failed. You can always come back to something later when you have more knowledge or better equipment and try again. I've done this and it worked!"

That was what happened with azathioprine. Robert Schwartz, a scientist at the New England Medical Center, remembered that the blood cells 6-mercaptopurine killed while fighting leukemia were like certain cells in the body's immune system. The immune system protects the body against disease by destroying "foreign" substances such as bacteria. Schwartz found he could use 6-mercaptopurine to keep the immune systems of rabbits from reacting to an injected foreign compound. The rabbits could still respond to other foreign substances later, however. Elion and Hitchings later found that 6-mercaptopurine had the same effect in mice—and azathioprine did the job even better.

The immune system helps the body most of the time. Sometimes, however, doctors want to keep the immune system from responding to a particular substance. One of these times is when

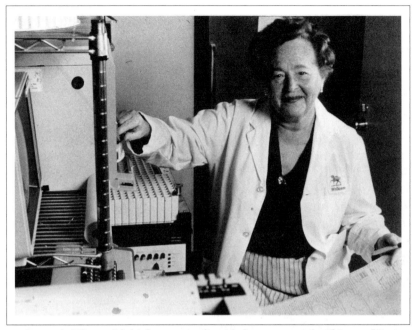

Gertrude Elion with high-pressure liquid chromatograph. This machine separates a solution into its different chemical parts. Elion uses it to find and measure the breakdown products of drugs in blood or urine.
(Courtesy Burroughs Wellcome Co.)

an organ, such as a kidney, is transplanted. The organ usually comes from someone who has died in an accident and has donated his or her organs to help others.

Unfortunately, the immune system cannot tell that a transplanted kidney can save a person's life. It "knows" only that the kidney comes from another body. Immune cells attack the "foreign" organ as if it were a dangerous microbe. If the immune system is not stopped, it will destroy the transplanted organ.

Roy Calne, a British transplant surgeon, heard about Schwartz's work. Calne decided to try giving 6-mercaptopurine to dogs receiving kidney transplants. Dogs given transplants without any drugs died after about 10 days. One dog that got 6-mercaptopurine, however, lived for 44 days.

Calne told Hitchings and Elion what he had found. Suddenly Elion remembered that azathioprine had blocked the immune systems of mice even better than 6-mercaptopurine did. She suggested that azathioprine might help the dogs' transplants last still longer.

Elion was right. Calne gave azathioprine to a collie named Lollipop, who then got a kidney transplant. Lollipop lived for 230 days with her new kidney. Even when she died, the kidney was still healthy.

Calne worked in the laboratory of a surgeon named Joseph Murray. After seeing azathioprine's success in Lollipop and other dogs, Murray decided to try the drug on human patients who needed a kidney transplant. He hoped it would allow the patients to accept kidneys from unrelated donors. Until that time, organ transplants in humans could take place only between identical twins. Identical twins have the same inherited information in their cells, so their immune systems do not see each other's tissue as foreign. In 1962, after two failures, Murray made a successful kidney transplant in a human patient by using azathioprine.

Azathioprine is still widely used to keep people's bodies from rejecting transplanted organs. Between 1965 and 1972 alone, 25,000 kidney transplants took place. Doctors were soon transplanting livers, lungs, and other organs as well, thanks largely to azathioprine. This drug was used in the first successful heart transplant.

Azathioprine also helps people with diseases in which the immune system attacks the person's own body. It is given to some people with the painful joint disease called rheumatoid arthritis, for example.

Gertrude Elion developed other important drugs during her long career. One, allopurinol, is used to treat another joint disease called gout. As with azathioprine, Elion found this drug while trying to improve 6-mercaptopurine.

Another drug, acyclovir, kills viruses of the herpes family. Herpesviruses cause some mild diseases such as cold sores and chicken pox. They can also cause more serious illnesses. One herpes disease can make people blind. Another infects the brain and can cause death. Acyclovir keeps the viruses from reproducing, much as 6-mercaptopurine does for cancer cells.

Elion points out that, as with azathioprine, finding acyclovir had an element of serendipity—discovering one thing while looking for something else. A good scientist never ignores unexpected results. Some of the best scientific ideas, Elion says, "are the result of trying to figure something out that puzzles you. You constantly are thinking over the results and asking, 'What does it mean?' and 'Why did it happen?'"

Elion and others in her lab found acyclovir by changing nucleic acids in a new way. Instead of changing the bases, as they had done to create 6-mercaptopurine, they modified the sugar molecules to which the bases were attached. One of these changes led to acyclovir. The "serendipity" element was that this chemical proved to be much more active against herpesviruses than related compounds were.

Howard Schaeffer, another Burroughs Wellcome researcher, first made acyclovir in 1974. Scientists in Wellcome's British laboratory then tested it against viruses. When the British scientists found that acyclovir kept herpesviruses from multiplying, Elion and others started studying how the compound worked and why it affected mainly that one virus family. "We worked out the whole metabolism," she says. She found out that the drug remains inactive until the virus changes it into another compound. That compound then poisons the virus. Other viruses do not change the drug in this way. Elion's work thus produced new knowledge about herpesviruses as well as a drug that could attack them.

Acyclovir "was a real breakthrough in antiviral research," Elion told an interviewer. "That such a thing was possible wasn't even imagined up till then." Burroughs Wellcome released the drug for human use in 1982. It is still the company's most profitable product. Later Elion's lab used similar techniques to develop AZT, the drug most commonly used to treat AIDS, although Elion herself did not work on this drug.

By the time Gertrude Elion worked on acyclovir, her life had changed. Since 1967 she had headed her own department at Burroughs Wellcome, the Department of Experimental Therapy. She also no longer lived in New York. In 1970 Burroughs Wellcome moved its headquarters to Research Triangle Park, North Carolina. Elion moved there, too.

Elion retired in 1983. She still came to her office each day, however. And, as it turned out, one of the greatest surprises of her career was yet to come.

On October 17, 1988, when Gertrude Elion was 70 years old, her telephone rang at 6:30 in the morning. She was already awake and dressing for work. "Congratulations," said the voice on the other end of the line. "You've won the Nobel Prize in medicine."

"You're kidding," Elion replied. Finally, however, the reporter who had called was able to persuade her that he was telling the truth. Along with George Hitchings, Elion really had received the same world-famous award that Maria Mayer had won (in a different category) 25 years earlier. Elion and Hitchings shared the award with a British drug researcher, Sir James W. Black.

The Nobel Prize usually goes to scientists who have done important basic research. Very rarely does the prize go to applied researchers such as drug developers. The Nobel committee said of Hitchings's and Elion's work, "While drug development had earlier mainly been built on chemical modification of natural products, they introduced a more rational approach based on the understanding of basic biochemical and physiological processes."

Elion was happy about the award, of course. "One is always pleased with recognition," she says, "and it was a recognition of a lot of work, a lifetime of work." But when she is asked if winning the prize was the high point of her career, she answers with a firm "No." As she explains, "The pleasure . . . that one got out of making useful drugs was something that really nothing can compare to. I still run into people who've had a kidney transplant for twenty years because of our drug. That is the kind of feeling that nothing else can come up to."

Gertrude Elion has received many awards and honors in addition to the Nobel Prize. In March 1991 she became the first woman to be included in the National Inventors Hall of Fame. (Drug developers are not often thought of as inventors, but Elion has 40 patents in her name.) She also received the National Medal of Science in 1991. She is included in the National Women's Hall of Fame and the Engineering and Science Hall of Fame.

Today, Gertrude Elion is so busy that her secretary is hard pressed to keep track of her calendar. "Everyone laughs when I say I'm retired, because I'm really doing just as much as before," Elion told a reporter at the time she won the Nobel Prize, and it is still true. She has served on many boards and committees, including the National Cancer Advisory Board and several committees connected with the World Health Organization. She also helps to train medical students at three nearby universities.

One of Elion's favorite tasks is giving lectures to young people, "trying to drum up more scientists." She says, "We've got to tell them how much fun it is. Everyone says it's hard work, but nobody says . . . how exciting it is to go in to work every day, and how you really don't want the weekend to come." Gertrude Elion shares both Helen Taussig's pleasure at helping sick people and Maria Mayer's joy in "working out" nature's puzzles. To Elion, both feelings are summed up in one simple word: "fun."

Chronology

January 23, 1918	Gertrude Elion born in New York City
1937	graduates with highest honors from Hunter College
1941	gets master's degree in chemistry from New York University
1944	joins Burroughs Wellcome Company
1951	develops 6-mercaptopurine
1962	first successful kidney transplant between unrelated donors is made with azathioprine
1967	Elion becomes head of department at Burroughs Wellcome
1974	acyclovir synthesized
1982	acyclovir released for human use
1983	Elion retires
October 1988	wins Nobel Prize in Physiology or Medicine
1991	wins National Medal of Science; becomes first woman elected to National Inventors Hall of Fame

Further Reading

Bouton, Katherine. "The Nobel Pair." *New York Times Magazine,* January 29, 1989. Longest biographical article about Elion and Hitchings.

The Cell: A Small Wonder. New York: Torstar, 1985. Gives background on nucleic acids and other parts of the cell.

Colburn, Don. "Pathway to the Prize." *Washington Post,* October 25, 1988. Provides background on Elion and how she did her Nobel Prize–winning work.

Elion, Gertrude B. "The Purine Path to Chemotherapy." *Science,* April 7, 1989. Elion's Nobel Prize lecture describes details of the work she did during her career. Difficult reading.

"Gertrude Belle Elion Is First Woman Elected to Inventors Hall of Fame." *Science Reports On File,* Facts On File, 1991. Brief article gives background on Elion's achievements and honors.

Holloway, Marguerite. "The Satisfaction of Delayed Gratification." *Scientific American,* October 1991. Good biographical article on Elion describes some of the frustrations she encountered.

Marx, Jean L. "The 1988 Nobel Prize for Physiology or Medicine." *Science,* October 28, 1988. Moderately technical article describes the achievements for which Elion, Hitchings, and Black were honored.

"Nobel Prize Scientists." *Coping,* 1989. Article offers biographical information about Elion and Hitchings.

Eugenie Clark
(1922–)

*Eugenie Clark. Clark wears the emblem of
the Russian submersible (small research
submarine)*Mir, *in which she made dives to
watch deep-sea sharks. She has also studied
other fish around the world.*
(Courtesy Andreas B. Rechnitzer)

*"T*hrough the crystal sea the monster came, heading directly
toward us. The mouth was so wide that the four of us . . . could
have slipped right into it. . . .

"Groping at the base of the dorsal [top] fin . . . I discovered a
soft cavity . . . and promptly dug my fingers into it. Then we were
off on a submarine voyage down the coast of Baja California. . . .
[Later] I pulled up my knees and sat astride the shark's great back
like a jockey."

In these words marine biologist Eugenie Clark described her first ride on a whale shark, the world's largest fish. She says this ride was the most exciting experience in her more than 50 years of exploring the undersea world.

What kind of person would ride on a shark? A person who understands sharks, for one thing. Clark knew that although some of the 370 known species of sharks are dangerous to humans, most are not. Even though the whale shark was over 50 feet long, it was harmless. Whale sharks eat only tiny animals that they filter out of sea water.

Eugenie Clark has done so much research with sharks that she has been nicknamed the "Shark Lady." But sharks are only one of the many kinds of fish she has studied. She has watched fish that glow in the dark, fish that change their sex in 10 seconds, and fish that disappear in the blink of an eye. She has discovered 11 species new to science and learned secrets of the behavior of many more. Her lively, popular writings have helped readers understand the sea and share her love for the amazing creatures that live in it.

Eugenie Clark was born May 4, 1922, in New York City. Her father, Charles Clark, an American of English and French ancestry, died when she was one year old. She was raised by her mother, uncle, and grandmother, who were Japanese-Americans.

After Eugenie's father died, her mother, Yumico, took many jobs to support the family. For awhile Yumico Clark was a swimming teacher. She took Eugenie to the beach and taught her to swim before Eugenie was two. Later, Mrs. Clark took care of a cigar and newspaper counter in the lobby of a New York club.

A working mother today might use the family television as a "babysitter." Yumico Clark had a more imaginative idea. She left Eugenie at the New York Aquarium during working hours on Saturday mornings.

This simple action opened a new world to nine-year-old Eugenie. "All about me were glass tanks with moving creatures in them," Clark wrote of this experience in her first book, *Lady with a Spear*.

At the back was a tank larger than the others, and the water in it was less clear, more mysterious. . . . A few feet from the glass wall that I looked through, it grew misty, as if there were no farther wall and the water just went on and on. . . . I brought my face as close as possible to the glass and pretended I was walking on the bottom of the sea.

Eugenie Clark

Eugenie waited eagerly for Saturdays. When Christmas came, she begged for an aquarium of her own. Yumico did not have much money, but she bought Eugenie a 15-gallon aquarium. As they picked out colorful fish to live in it, Mrs. Clark became almost as excited as her daughter. By the time they left the store they had spent the allowance for more future birthdays and Christmases than they could count.

It was no surprise that Eugenie Clark majored in zoology, or the study of animals, when she went to Hunter College in New York City. (Gertrude Elion had graduated from Hunter the year before Clark started there.) Clark planned to become an ichthyologist—a scientist who studies fish. When she graduated in 1942, however, the only job she could find was as a chemist at a plastics company. Again like Elion, Clark took graduate courses at New York University at night. She received a master's degree and later, in 1950, a Ph.D.

Clark did her first equipment diving in 1947, when she was doing part-time research at the Scripps Institute of Oceanography in La Jolla, California. Scuba gear had not yet been invented, so Clark had to wear a heavy helmet with a hose attached to an air pump. After she had been on the sea floor a while, she began to have trouble breathing. She almost fainted before she could slip out of the helmet and swim to the surface. Back on the boat, she found that a mending job on her hose had failed. Most of the air had leaked out of the hose before reaching her. Clark refused to let this frightening experience ruin diving for her, however. After a short rest while the hose was repaired, she dived again—and had no further trouble.

Beginning in June 1949, Eugenie Clark spent four months in the South Pacific collecting fish in a study sponsored by the U.S. Navy and the Pacific Science Board. She visited islands such as Kwajalein, Guam, Saipan, and the Palaus. These islands were part of a trust territory that the United Nations had given to the United States to administer after World War II. The navy wanted to know which fish in the area were poisonous to eat.

Clark worked with each island's best fishermen. She collected fish from shallow tidepools by pouring a poison into the water. The poison stunned or killed the fish, making them easy to pick up. Using it let Clark gather a wide variety of fish quickly without damaging their bodies. In deeper water she captured small fish in glass jars and collected larger ones by spearing them. She spent some nights in native houses built on stilts and learned to eat raw squid, raw shark, and the muscles of giant clams.

In 1950 Clark obtained a Fulbright scholarship to study fishes in the Red Sea. This 1,000-mile-long, cigar-shaped body of water lies between the northeastern coast of Africa and the Arabian peninsula. Clark thinks it may be named for the deep pink light reflected into it from nearby mountains at sunrise and sunset. The Red Sea is part of the tropical Indian and Pacific oceans, but it is almost completely cut off from these waters. Clark calls it "unique among seas." About 20 percent of its plants and animals live nowhere else. The Red Sea's ocean life is more closely related to that around Hawaii, 12,000 miles away, than to the sea life in the temperate Mediterranean Sea just to the north.

Beginning in January 1951, Clark studied Red Sea fish for nine months at a small marine station called Ghardaqa, on the coast of Egypt. Once again she focused on poisonous fishes. She collected 300 species of fish, including about 40 poisonous ones and 3 species new to science. Clark usually went to sea in the mornings, then spent the afternoons and evenings in the lab. She dissected (cut up) and preserved her specimens and wrote down what she had seen.

Before Clark left New York for the Red Sea she had begun dating a young Greek-born doctor named Ilias Papakonstantinou. Ilias shared her interest in the sea. Unlike other men she had dated, he was not afraid of "play[ing] second fiddle to a fish." In June 1951 Ilias came to visit Eugenie. They were married in a Greek Orthodox church in Cairo. They spent their honeymoon on the Red Sea, where Clark taught her new husband how to spearfish.

Clark returned to New York to work at the American Museum of Natural History. Hera, the first of her four children, was born in 1952. In that same year she received a grant to write a popular book describing her adventures in the South Pacific and on the Red Sea. The book, *Lady with a Spear*, was published in 1953. Its lively style made it popular even with people who had never thought of fish except as something to have for dinner. Like Grace Hopper, Clark knew how to make science interesting to nonscientists.

Among the people who enjoyed Clark's book were a wealthy couple named William H. and Anne Vanderbilt. They and William Vanderbilt's brother Alfred owned a large tract of land on Florida's west coast. In 1954 the Vanderbilts told Clark that they wanted to build a marine biology laboratory on this land. They asked her to be its director.

Clark was delighted. The site was excellent, and little was known about the sea life that swam in that part of the Gulf of Mexico.

The move fitted in well with her family's plans, too. Ilias had just finished his medical training and liked the idea of setting up his practice in Florida.

Eugenie Clark and her family arrived to open the Cape Haze Marine Laboratory in early January 1955. The family now included a newborn second daughter, Aya. The equally newborn laboratory consisted of a small wooden building with shelves for specimens and a sink. The only other facility was a dock for Alfred Vanderbilt's boat, which the lab could borrow.

Clark's most important work at the Cape Haze laboratory was the study of living sharks. She kept them in a pen near the boat dock. The pen was just a fenced-in part of the sea.

In the summer of 1958 Lester Aronson, an expert on animal psychology, visited the lab. "Has anyone ever made a study of the learning behavior of sharks?" he asked Clark.

It seemed that no one had. Most zoologists assumed that sharks were just big, stupid eating machines. Clark suspected they were wrong.

Clark decided to try to train two nine-foot lemon sharks that lived in the shark pen. She made a square wooden "target" and painted it white. At feeding time she lowered the target into the shark pen and dangled a piece of fish from it on a string. A shark had to bump the target with its nose to get the fish.

The target was connected to a doorbell sealed in a metal cylinder. When the shark bumped the target, the bell rang. If the shark could be trained to associate the sound of the bell with food, it would bump the target and ring the bell even when food was not present. Animals such as pigeons and rats learn this kind of task easily. Aronson warned Clark, however, that the sharks might take months to do it.

In fact they needed only days. For six weeks Clark trained the sharks to take food while bumping the target and ringing the bell. Then she gave them the "big test": she put the target in the water but attached no food to it. At first the sharks swam past the target. On the 10th pass, however, the male nuzzled the target and rang the bell. Clark immediately dropped some food fish into the water. Within three days both sharks butted the target regularly to get their fishy rewards.

Clark then made the task harder. She required the sharks to push the target, then make a sharp turn and swim to the other end of the pen within 10 seconds to get their reward. They learned that trick, too. In fact, the female shark learned something that Clark

Nurse sharks. Adult nurse sharks are almost blind, but young ones can see well. One baby nurse shark was the brightest "pupil" Eugenie Clark ever had in her shark training tests.
(Courtesy Special Collections, California Academy of Sciences)

had not intended to teach. The female found that if she waited in the feeding area while the male pushed the target, she could get the reward fish before the male had time to swim over to it!

Clark continued her shark training experiments during her 12 years at the Cape Haze lab. She tried targets of different colors, shapes, and patterns. She also trained several kinds of sharks. Her experiments showed that sharks were more intelligent than anyone had thought. She considers these experiments her most important scientific work.

The more Clark learned about sharks, the more respect she had for them—and the less fear. Many times she has tried to ease other people's fear of these "magnificent and misunderstood" animals. "Unless provoked or threatened they prefer to retreat rather than to challenge anything as large as man," she has written. She does not deny that some sharks, such as the great white shark and the tiger shark, can be dangerous to humans. She maintains, however, that stories and movies such as *Jaws* greatly exaggerate the danger. "You have a better chance of being hit by a car when you leave your house than [of] being attacked by a shark when you go swimming," she says.

Sharks were not the only fish that Clark studied during her years at Cape Haze. She was just as excited about certain small members of the sea bass or grouper family. When she first saw these fish, she noticed many females with their bellies swollen with eggs—but she could spot no males.

In time Clark learned the answer to the grouper mystery: the fish could change sex! Each fish has the organs to be both male and female. Some other fish can change sex, but few can be both sexes at once. If this grouper is separated from others of its kind, it can fertilize its own eggs.

More often, the groupers take turns fertilizing each other. During the mating process they can switch sex in just 10 seconds. Clark knows of no other fish that can make the change so fast. She thinks these unspectacular-looking fish are the most interesting marine creatures she has studied.

Clark added two sons to her family while she was at Cape Haze. Tak came along in 1956 and Niki in 1958. Not surprisingly, all of Clark's children learned to swim before they could walk. They often went with their mother on fishing and diving expeditions.

The Cape Haze lab grew, too. New buildings were added. In 1960 the lab moved to Siesta Key, in Sarasota, Florida. This made life easier for Clark and her husband, who worked at the hospital in Sarasota.

Clark's marriage to Ilias Papakonstantinou ended in 1967. She also decided to leave the Cape Haze laboratory at that time. She turned it over to a new director, Perry Gilbert. The lab gained a new sponsor, William R. Mote, and was renamed the Mote Marine Laboratory.

In 1968 Clark joined the University of Maryland, where she still teaches. She also wrote a second book, *The Lady and the Sharks*, which described her years at the Cape Haze laboratory. It was published in 1969.

Clark now once again had the freedom to travel and dive all over the world. She used that freedom to make many discoveries about undersea life during the 1970s and 1980s. Two of the most unusual ones were the Moses sole and the "sleeping" sharks.

The Moses sole is a small flatfish that lives on the bottom of the Red Sea. Its top is speckled like the sand it hides in, but it is white underneath. A legend says that when Moses parted the Red Sea, a fish was cut in half. The two halves became the first Moses soles.

The truth about the Moses sole is stranger than any legend. Clark first saw the fish near Elat, Israel, in 1960. When she caught one, she noticed a few drops of milky fluid oozing from pores on its fins. "The milk felt slippery and caused a tightening sensation in my fingers," she wrote in a 1974 article. "I suspected it might be poisonous."

Clark returned to the Red Sea in 1972 and 1973 to study the Moses sole further. She found that no big fish, not even a shark, would touch the little flatfish. When a shark tried to swallow the sole, she wrote, "the deadly predator jerked away, its jaws 'frozen' open. Vigorously shaking its head, . . . the shark dashed around the pool . . . before at last succeeding in closing its mouth." If Clark wiped a sole with alcohol to remove its protective milk, however, the sole "was inside a shark's stomach in a flash."

Clark reports that "a thimbleful of this substance . . . will keep away hungry sharks for as long as 22 hours." The fluid cannot be made into a commercial shark repellent, however, because it breaks down quickly at room temperature. Clark is not sorry. "I really don't think one needs a shark repellent," she says.

The sole's "milk" is a powerful poison as well as a repellent. It kills small fish instantly. The poison does not harm the sole, however, because the sole carries an antidote that stops the poison's action. This antidote or inhibitor interests Clark more than the poison. She and other researchers have found that the inhibitor stops the action of the venom of scorpions, bees, and some poisonous snakes as well as of the Moses sole poison. The inhibitor must be put into the blood at the same time as the poison, though. This means it probably could not be used as, say, a treatment for snakebite. It may help scientists learn more about how such poisons work, however.

Just as strange as the Moses sole are the "sleeping" sharks. Clark heard from a diving friend that sharks crowded into certain underwater caves on Mexico's Yucatan Peninsula. They stayed there quietly, seemingly in a trance. Divers could sometimes touch and even lift the sharks gently without getting much response.

Clark first saw the sharks for herself in 1973. One female "stood still as if for inspection. . . . Her eyes were open. . . . Her mouth opened and closed rhythmically." Clark found that the sharks in the cave belonged to the family of requiem sharks. Many of the most dangerous sharks, including reef sharks and tiger sharks, are part of this family.

The mystery of the sleeping sharks still has not been solved. Clark found some tantalizing clues, however. For one thing, she learned that rain water seeps up into the caves from underground streams. The water in the caves therefore can become less salty than normal sea water. Clark remembered that when she had an aquarium as a child, she sometimes put her fish briefly in fresh water to rid them of tiny parasites on their skins. For some reason the fresh water made the irritating parasites fall off. Sharks also get parasites, but the sharks in the caves seemed to have far fewer than other sharks. Clark wondered if the water in the caves made the parasites loosen their hold on the sharks.

Small fish called remoras hovered around the big sharks in the caves. These fish often swim with sharks. Clark saw that the remoras in the caves were picking parasites off the sharks' gills. Their job was easy because the sharks were holding still instead of swimming constantly as sharks usually do. The sharks might have learned that they could come to these caves and be cleaned of parasites by the combination of fresh water and remoras. Clark later found similar "sleeping shark" caves off the coast of Japan.

Clark has studied many other kinds of sharks and other fish. She has dived down 12,000 feet in a submersible (small research submarine) to observe deep-sea sharks. In waters off Western Australia she spotted 20 rare whale sharks in one day and rode on 11 of them. In the Red Sea, to which she has returned over 40 times, she has studied fish with patches under their eyes that glow in the dark. She has also observed snakelike eels that rise from their sandy burrows like plants in a garden. She has spent time in both the Red Sea's fish-filled coral reefs and its bare sandy areas, which she calls "the desert beneath the sea."

Clark has changed her methods of studying fish since the days when she collected them with spears and poison. In 1990 she signed a copy of her first book, *Lady with a Spear*, by writing, "Lady Without a Spear Now." She said that she and a fellow scientist have promised each other that "we're not going to kill fish any-more." Clark has also worked to get rich undersea worlds preserved as parks. For example, she was part of a group that persuaded the government of Egypt to make Ras Muhammad, an "underwater fairyland" at the southern tip of the Sinai Peninsula, Egypt's first national park.

Clownfish and sea anemone in the Red Sea at Ras Muhammad, Egypt. Curiosity about the relationship between these fish and their flowerlike animal companion first brought Eugenie Clark to the Red Sea. Later she helped to persuade the Egyptian government to make the "underwater fairyland" of Ras Muhammad a national park. (Courtesy Egyptian Tourist Authority, Los Angeles)

Eugenie Clark retired from the University of Maryland in 1992. She still keeps her office and a laboratory there, however, and teaches one class a year. Although she is now over 70 years old, she has no plans to stop diving. "It's one of the few sports or activities you can do when you're any age," she says. "The buoyancy underwater is wonderful for all your joint problems." As she told one interviewer, "I plan to keep on diving and researching and conserving until I'm at least ninety years old."

When interviewed for this book in early 1993, Clark was on her way to Papua New Guinea, a group of islands north of Australia. She wants to compare tilefish that swim off New Guinea with tilefish she has studied in the Red Sea and the Caribbean. These small fish build burrows in the sand, then pile bits of coral and other debris on top of them. Some burrows in the Caribbean are over eight feet across. Clark wants to find out why the fish make their "roofs" so large. She also wants to learn why the males of some species of tilefish have harems with many females, while those of other species have only one mate. It is clear that her fascination with sea life, born so long ago in the halls of the New York Aquarium, has never decreased—and undoubtedly never will.

Chronology

May 4, 1922	Eugenie Clark born in New York City
1931	first visits New York Aquarium
1942	graduates from Hunter College
1947	does first diving with helmet and face mask
1949	collects fish in South Pacific
1950	collects fish in Red Sea; receives Ph.D. degree from New York University
1951	marries Ilias Papakonstantinou
1953	publishes *Lady with a Spear*
1955–67	heads Cape Haze Marine Laboratory; trains sharks, studies groupers and other fish
1967	leaves Cape Haze Marine Laboratory; divorced from Ilias Papakonstantinou
1968	joins University of Maryland
1969	publishes *The Lady and the Sharks*
1972–73	studies Moses sole
1973	studies "sleeping" sharks
1970–present	studies fish that glow in the dark, garden eels, tilefish, and many others

Further Reading

"Clark, Eugenie." *Current Biography,* 1953. Sketch of Clark's early career, written soon after *Lady with a Spear* was published.

Clark, Eugenie. "Into the Lairs of 'Sleeping' Sharks." *National Geographic,* April 1975. Describes Clark's dives in caves off Mexico's Yucatan Peninsula.

_____. *The Lady and the Sharks.* New York: Harper & Row, 1969. Account of Clark's 12 years as director of the Cape Haze Marine Laboratory.

_____. *Lady with a Spear.* New York: Harper & Row, 1953. Describes Clark's early adventures collecting fish in the South Pacific and the Red Sea.

_____. "The Red Sea's Sharkproof Fish." *National Geographic,* November 1974. Tells how the Moses sole repels sharks.

_____. "Sharks: Magnificent and Misunderstood." *National Geographic,* August 1981. Presents recent research on sharks and contradicts myths about their danger to humans.

_____. "Whale Sharks, Gentle Monsters of the Sea." *National Geographic,* December 1992. Clark's most recent *National Geographic* article describes seeing 20 whale sharks in one day off Western Australia.

Facklam, Margery. *Wild Animals, Gentle Women.* New York: Harcourt Brace Jovanovich, 1978. For young adults. Devotes a chapter to Clark, focusing on her "sleeping shark" research.

Labastille, Anne. *Women and Wilderness.* San Francisco: Sierra Club Books, 1980. Devotes a chapter to an interview with Clark.

Phinizy, Coles. "Lovely Lady with a Very Fishy Reputation." *Sports Illustrated,* October 4, 1965. Biographical article describes Clark at about mid-career.

Jewel Plummer Cobb
(1924–)

*Jewel Plummer Cobb. Cobb has been successful in three
different careers: cancer research, teaching,
and college administration.*
(Courtesy Jewel Plummer Cobb)

---

*L*aTonya is a young African-American woman. As a child, she had
cancer. Chemotherapy drugs saved her life. Inspired by the doctors who helped her, LaTonya decided that she wanted to do
cancer research when she grew up.

When LaTonya's older brother went to high school, the only
science class offered was a general one. By the time LaTonya was

a freshman, however, her school had started a program to help students interested in science prepare for courses in college. The program helped LaTonya's school prepare excellent biology and chemistry classes for interested students.

Now LaTonya is going to school at California State College in Fullerton. She lives in the Jewel Plummer Cobb Residence Halls. LaTonya never dreams that she owes her place to live, the classes that got her into college, and perhaps even her life to the woman whose name she sees every morning as she leaves the residence hall to go to class.

LaTonya is imaginary, but Jewel Plummer Cobb's achievements are not. Cobb has been successful in three careers: medical research, teaching, and university administration. She has improved understanding of cancer and anticancer drugs, taught at several colleges and been the president of one, and started programs that help minority students prepare for scientific careers.

Jewel Plummer was born in Chicago on January 17, 1924. She came from a family with a history of interest in science. Her grandfather trained as a pharmacist, and her father, Frank V. Plummer, was a medical doctor. Many of his patients were African-Americans who worked in the Chicago stockyards. He located his office near a streetcar transfer point so these workers could visit him easily.

Young Jewel, an only child, enjoyed talking with her father "about science things at the dinner table." She also liked looking through his extensive home library. Her own interest in science did not begin, however, until high school. Before then she thought she might follow the career of her mother, Carriebel. Carriebel Cole Plummer taught dance and physical education in Chicago schools.

Jewel Plummer's love of science started in a biology class, when she looked through a microscope for the first time. She still remembers that moment. "It was really awe-inspiring," she says. "I said, 'My goodness, here's a world that I never even knew about! Wow!'"

Jewel got a B.A. in biology from Talledega College in Alabama in 1944. Then, like Gertrude Elion and Eugenie Clark, she went to New York University for graduate work. But whereas Elion learned about the chemicals of life and Clark learned about whole animals, Plummer was most fascinated by individual cells. Using the microscope to guide her, she learned how to perform delicate surgery on cells. Plummer gained her Master's degree in 1947 and her Ph.D. in 1950. She also got her first taste of teaching as a graduate teaching fellow during these years.

After getting her advanced degrees, Plummer joined a research team at the Cancer Research Foundation of Harlem Hospital in New York City. Jane Wright, an African-American medical researcher and physician, was the team's leader. The group studied the effects of different anticancer drugs on human cancer cells. Wright took cells from people with advanced cancer, and Plummer grew the cells in tissue culture. She kept them in test tube cultures or flasks and provided them with nutrients. In addition to studying the cells under a microscope, Cobb made time-lapse movies to show how the cells changed after being treated with various drugs.

Chemotherapy, or drug treatment for cancer, was new in those days. For example, 6-mercaptopurine, the anticancer drug Gertrude Elion discovered, had just been introduced. Predicting whether a particular drug would affect a certain kind of cancer or what dose of drug should be used was hard. The Cancer Research Foundation group hoped to find a way to test different drugs on cells from a person's cancer to find the most effective drug and dose. Then doctors would not have to give the drugs to the person in a hit-or-miss way.

Unfortunately, Wright and Plummer found that they could not predict drugs' behavior dependably on the basis of their cell experiments. Their predictions were correct for some drugs and some cancers but not for others. Their work was not wasted, however. Their observations of changes in cells exposed to these drugs helped future researchers. Indeed, Jewel Plummer Cobb says she is prouder of this work than of any other research she did.

Plummer's work revealed facts about anticancer drugs that had not been known before. For example, she learned that a drug named actinomycin D affected a part of the cell called the nucleolus. Later researchers, following up her work, found that actinomycin D damaged the RNA in the nucleolus. RNA (ribonucleic acid) is a chemical relative of the DNA (deoxyribonucleic acid) that Gertrude Elion worked with. Both are nucleic acids. RNA translates the inherited instructions in the DNA into blueprints that tell a cell how to make particular chemicals. Plummer's research helped scientists understand cancer better. Like Elion's, it also helped in developing more effective chemotherapy drugs.

Jewel Plummer left the Cancer Research Foundation in 1952. She then taught at the University of Illinois for two years. In 1954 she married Roy Cobb, an insurance salesman. They had a son, Jonathan, in 1957. Jewel Plummer Cobb joined the faculty of Sarah Lawrence College in Bronxville, New York, in 1960. In addition to raising Jonathan, Cobb did research and taught biology.

Cobb's research at Sarah Lawrence centered on skin cells containing a dark pigment (coloring material) called melanin. Melanin gives human skin its color. Some groups, such as most people of African ancestry, have large amounts of melanin in their skin. Usually the ancestors of these groups lived in hot climates, where they were exposed to strong sunlight.

Cobb, among others, found that melanin can protect skin cells from damage caused by radiation. Radiation, including the ultraviolet radiation in sunlight, can damage the nucleic acids in cells. It sometimes makes the cells cancerous. Cobb suspected that dark skins developed in sunny climates as a way of partly protecting people against skin cancer.

In addition to studying normal melanin-containing cells, Cobb studied cells from a skin cancer called malignant melanoma. Melanoma produces dark tumors, even in light-skinned people, because melanoma cells contain large amounts of melanin. Unlike the most common kind of skin cancer, which is easily treated, melanoma grows quickly and is often fatal. Cobb did not find any new treatments for melanoma, but she learned important facts about the biology of melanoma cells.

In 1969, Jewel Plummer Cobb became dean of Connecticut College in New London. She thus began her third career, that of college administrator, in addition to going on with teaching and research. She and Roy Cobb had been divorced in 1967, so she was then the single mother of a 12-year-old boy. Keeping up with all these different parts of her life required "quite a . . . fast pace."

Cobb's days at Connecticut College started early and ended late. "I [went] to my lab every morning at eight o'clock and work[ed] with my two research assistants . . . till ten," she recalls. "Then I went over to my dean's office and began work there." She taught in the afternoon. Cobb felt it was important to do her laboratory work first, because the administrative work was "an endless process . . . paper, paper, paper." She and her son relaxed and

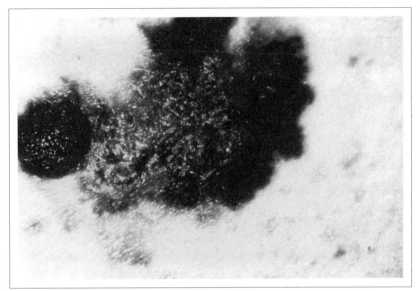

Malignant melanoma tumor. Jewel Cobb's research helped scientists
understand this fast-growing, deadly skin cancer.
(Courtesy Skin Cancer Foundation, New York, N.Y.)

enjoyed time together by going to Vermont to ski every weekend in winter.

In time the "fast pace" became too much to handle, and Jewel Cobb was forced to make some hard choices. "Research required a great deal of time," she notes. "Sometimes in the middle of the night you had to do certain things in the lab." Reluctantly she decided to give up research in favor of teaching, because she found that she liked to "be with students all the time."

Cobb became dean of Douglass College, the women's college of Rutgers University in New Jersey, in 1976. "The Douglass College deanship is like being a president because you [have] your own campus and your own faculty," she says.

It was perhaps no surprise, then, that Cobb received a letter in 1981 suggesting that she apply for the presidency of California State University at Fullerton. Cal State Fullerton, as it is known, had over 1,000 faculty members and served some 24,000 students at that time. Cobb got the job, even though the California state university system had had only two other woman college presidents before then. She was the first African-American woman to head a major public university on the West Coast.

The Fullerton campus was located in a conservative community, and most of its students were white. Still, Cobb says she did not encounter any overt criticism because she was an African American or a woman. On the contrary, she has reported that she "had a positive reception" from the beginning. She does feel, however, that it took quite a while for members of the college and community to "realize that I [had] the experience and the diplomacy" to do a good job.

Cobb made her own work as president of Cal State Fullerton harder "because I elected to be both an internal and an external president." This meant that in addition to running the campus, she became very involved in community activities. Like other leaders of state universities, she also spent a lot of time talking to state legislators. She had to persuade them to grant money for new buildings and other things that she felt the college needed.

Cobb set a number of goals for herself and the university and accomplished them "quite well," she says. She established two new schools, both dealing with subjects very important in the modern world: the School of Communication and the School of Engineering and Computer Science. She shared an interest in these fields with Grace Hopper. Cobb also persuaded the California legislature to give the university several new buildings, including a new science building, a new engineering wing, a new center for gerontology (the study of old age), and the university's first residence hall. Before Cobb's time, the university had been totally a "commuter campus," with no place for students to live. Cobb, however, felt that living on campus "is a very important part of the learning process" for students. The residence hall bears her name.

Jewel Cobb retired from the presidency of Cal State Fullerton in 1990, but she has remained a trustee professor in the California State University system. This is a "portable" position, which means that Cobb can work at any campus in the system. She has chosen to have her office at Cal State Los Angeles, a campus strongly concerned with college preparation in math and science for minorities.

Helping minority students prepare for college is Cobb's main activity these days. She heads a center, sponsored by the National Science Foundation, that develops precollege programs to increase the number of minority students interested in math and science. One program helps junior high school teachers learn new

The Jewel Plummer Cobb Residence Halls at California State University, Fullerton. Cobb established the university's first residence halls while she was president of Cal State Fullerton.
(Courtesy Patrick B. O'Donnell and California State University, Fullerton)

ways to make math and science exciting for students. Another helps high school students "who have been low or modest achievers" prepare for college and for science careers. "Education is still the best pathway" for minorities to follow in trying to achieve equality, Cobb believes.

An earlier program that helped students become scientists is what Cobb names as her greatest achievement. She established this program while she was dean of Connecticut College. The program was for students who had decided late in their college careers that they wanted to become medical doctors or dentists. Many of these students were minorities. Because they made their decision late, they did not have time before they graduated to take the science courses required for medical or dental school. Their careers might have come to a stop at this point if it had not been for Cobb's program. The program paid the students' tuition while they made up the science courses they needed. Cobb says proudly that 85 percent of these students were accepted at medical or dental schools. "They are now doctors and dentists, and I'm very happy about that." Programs based on Cobb's have been set up at over 20 other colleges.

Jewel Cobb has written almost 50 publications. Most describe her scientific research, but some discuss problems facing minorities and/or women. She has received honorary degrees from 18 colleges or universities. She is a member of the Institute of Medicine of the National Research Council, and her photograph hangs in the National Academy of Sciences building in Washington, D.C. She was also awarded the Douglass Medal by Douglass College.

All of Cobb's careers have been rewarding for her. She is pleased with her record in administration. She says it shows her ability to "have some vision about new programs and then . . . work with faculty or staff and have them take on the project[s] as their own."

Teaching excites Cobb even more. "You can see the electric light go on when kids understand what you're talking about," she says. She told one interviewer that she wants to be remembered as "a Black woman scientist who cared very much about what happens to young folks, particularly women going into science." Her advice to such women is "Reach for the stars—and don't stop!"

Cobb's favorite of all her careers, though, is the one she had to give up: research. "It's . . . never the same every day. . . . [You have to choose] what . . . questions you want to ask, what . . . challenges [to handle] in doing the experiments, find out what the data is, write it up." She says biological science is "the most exciting field in the world." As far as Cobb is concerned, a blend of teaching and research, along with family life, makes the ideal career.

Jewel Plummer Cobb's research on cancer has led, indirectly at least, to saving lives. In this she is like Gertrude Elion and Helen

Taussig. She has studied cells as carefully as Flossie Wong-Staal later studied viruses. But the achievements Cobb remembers best involve saving lives in a different sense—turning young minds, especially those of minority students, toward the fruitful path of study and research that has rewarded her so well.

Chronology

January 17, 1924	Jewel Plummer born in Chicago
1944	graduates from Talledega College in biology
1950	gets Ph.D. from New York University
1950–52	does research on anticancer drugs at Cancer Research Foundation
1952–54	teaches at University of Illinois
1954	marries Roy Cobb
1960	moves to Sarah Lawrence; teaches and does research on cells containing melanin
1967	divorced from Roy Cobb
1969	becomes dean of Connecticut College
1976	becomes dean of Douglass College; gives up research
1981	becomes president of California State University at Fullerton
1990	retires from Cal State Fullerton presidency; becomes trustee professor at Cal State Los Angeles

Further Reading

Cobb, Jewel. "Filters for Women in Science." *Annals of the New York Academy of Sciences*, v. 323, 1979. Claims that women are "filtered out" of many science jobs that are available to men; calls for new programs to interest girls and women in science.

Irvin, Dona L. "Jewell Plummer Cobb." In Jessie Carney Smith, ed., *Epic Lives: One Hundred Black Women Who Made a Difference*. Detroit: Visible Ink Press/Gale Research Inc., 1993. The most complete biographical profile of Cobb.

"Shaper of Young Minds." *Ebony*, August 1982. Focuses on Cobb's work as president of California State University at Fullerton; also provides background information on her.

Yount, Lisa. *Black Scientists*. New York: Facts On File, 1991. For young adults. Chapter on Jane Wright provides information about the work that Wright and Plummer did at the Cancer Research Foundation and about the development of chemotherapy for cancer.

Vera Cooper Rubin
(1928–)

*Vera Cooper Rubin. Rubin's observations of
the motions of galaxies showed that up to 90
percent of the universe is made of matter we
can't see.*
(Courtesy Mark Godfrey)

*I*n 1938 a 10-year-old girl lay in her bed in Washington, D.C.,
watching the night sky. The thing young Vera Cooper liked best
about the house she and her family had just moved into was the
view from her bedroom window. Her bed was right under the
north-facing window, and for hours—sometimes all night
long—she stared at the stars as they appeared to move slowly
across the sky. "I just couldn't look at the sky without wondering
how anyone could do anything but study the stars," Vera Cooper
Rubin recalls.

The movement Vera saw each night was caused by the turning
of the earth. But the stars really do move, and Vera Rubin is still

watching them. Now she does it with the help of telescopes and computers. By studying the movement of the huge groups of stars called galaxies, Rubin has made discoveries that changed scientists' view of the universe as completely as Maria Mayer's insights changed their view of atoms. Rubin's measurements have shown that up to 90 percent of the universe is made of matter no one can see.

Vera Cooper was born in Philadelphia, Pennsylvania, on July 23, 1928. Her father, Philip, was an electrical engineer. Rose, her mother, worked for Bell Telephone Company for a while before quitting to raise her two daughters. At bedtime Vera's mother used to scold her, "Don't spend all night hanging out the window!" Still, when the Coopers realized their daughter's interest in astronomy was serious, they encouraged it. Vera's father helped her build a telescope when she was 14.

Vera chose Vassar, in Poughkeepsie, New York, as her college partly because Maria Mitchell, a famous woman astronomer, had taught there. Vera graduated in 1948 with excellent grades, but she still had a limited choice of graduate schools. Princeton wouldn't even send her a catalog because their graduate school didn't admit women.

While she was still at Vassar, Vera Cooper met a young physicist from Cornell University named Robert Rubin. They were married in 1948, just after Vera graduated. Vera had applied for a scholarship for graduate school at Harvard. Still, with what she now says was "very little thought," she joined Bob Rubin at Cornell in Ithaca, New York. In those days, most working couples assumed that the man's career was more important than the woman's.

Cornell's astronomy department at that time consisted of just two professors. That didn't stop Vera Rubin from getting her Master's degree there in 1951—or from making a discovery so startling that at first no one believed it.

In the years just before Vera Rubin was born, astronomers' picture of the universe changed dramatically. An astronomer named Edwin Hubble showed that some of what had been called nebulae ("clouds") were actually huge clusters of stars. These star clusters were named galaxies. The band of light that people call the Milky Way is the star-packed disk of the galaxy that contains our solar system.

A device called a spectrograph can be used to study how stars and galaxies move. An astronomer attaches a spectrograph to a big telescope and focuses the telescope on, say, a star. Light from the star passes through a slit in the spectrograph and is spread out into a spectrum, or rainbow. If a photographic plate is put behind the spectrograph, the spectrum can be photographed. Spectra (plural of *spectrum*) of galaxies are made the same way.

The light from the "burning" of each chemical element in a star makes its own pattern of lines on a spectrum. Astronomers know where the lines for each element fall in spectra made on earth. Because of what is called the Doppler effect, all the lines in a star's light pattern are shifted toward the red end of the spectrum if the star is moving away from the earth. They are shifted toward the blue end if the star is moving toward the earth. By measuring the shift, astronomers can determine the speed of the star's movement. Again, the same is true of galaxies.

In the 1920s, astronomers discovered red shifts in almost all the galaxy spectra that had been made. This suggested that all the galaxies were moving away from earth and from each other. In other words, the universe was expanding or spreading out.

Some astronomers suggested that this was happening because the universe had begun in an unimaginable explosion 10 to 20 billion years ago. All the matter left from this "big bang" had been flying outward ever since. Around 1950, when Vera Rubin was studying at Cornell, astronomers were just beginning to accept the big bang theory. Most still believe in some form of it.

Still following her interest in the movement of the heavens, Rubin wondered whether galaxies were moving relative to each other in any way besides that described by the expanding universe. "It was awfully early to be asking that question, but I didn't know enough to realize that," Rubin says now.

Spectra had been made for only about a hundred galaxies at that time. When Rubin analyzed these spectra, she found that galaxies of the same apparent brightness (which, astronomers assumed, were about the same distance from earth) seemed to be moving faster in some parts of the sky than others. This extra motion suggested that the galaxies might be rotating around an unknown center, the way the planets rotate around the sun in our solar system. At the time, however, no astronomical theory could explain why galaxies should do such a thing.

One day in 1950, Bob and Vera Rubin drove through the snow to Philadelphia. Their month-old son, David, was with them. Vera went to a meeting of the American Astronomical Society in the city. There, in a 10-minute talk, she presented her findings about the galaxies' strange motion.

Rubin was only 22 years old, a stranger from a small astronomy department, and a woman to boot—and she was claiming results no one could explain. Perhaps it was no wonder that she was all but politely hooted off the stage. Her report "got an enormous amount of publicity, almost all negative," she says. "But at least," she adds wryly, "from then on, astronomers knew who I was."

Bob Rubin got a job with the National Bureau of Standards, and the family moved back to Washington, D.C. Vera's parents still lived there.

Vera stayed home at first to take care of her new baby. Much as she loved David, she found she was not happy as a full-time mother. "Nothing in my education had taught me that one year after Cornell my husband would be out doing his science and I would be home changing diapers," she recalls. For about a year her only contact with astronomy was the *Astrophysical Journal*. Each time she opened a new issue, she burst into tears.

Bob Rubin urged Vera to go on to get her doctor's degree. She signed up at Georgetown University, the only college in the area with a Ph.D. program in astronomy. But by then life had become even more complicated: the Rubins had a new daughter, Judith, in addition to David.

Getting Vera Rubin to evening classes at Georgetown required a juggling act even more amazing than the one Jewel Cobb did later at Connecticut College. Rubin, her husband, and both her parents took part. The act was doubly hard because neither Vera nor her mother could drive.

"My husband would leave work and pick up my mother," Rubin remembers. "He would bring her to our house. She would come with supper for my father. I would have fed the children, and I would get in the car with my husband's supper. He would drive me to Georgetown and just sit in the parking lot and eat and work or read while I was in school. Meanwhile my father would leave his office and then come to our house. . . . We did that two nights a week for about a year. It was a . . . three-ring circus."

Perhaps not surprisingly, Vera Rubin decided to do her Ph.D. project on something completely different from the subject of her ill-received master's thesis. "The heated controversy really spoiled the fun" of doing astronomy, she says. "My way of handling that, in every case, has just been to go off and do something very different."

Rubin's Ph.D. thesis tried to describe mathematically the distribution of galaxies in the local part of the universe. "My entire . . . thesis consisted of essentially one very long calculation," she says. Today a computer could do that calculation in minutes. In the early 1950s, however, Rubin had to work with a desktop calculator, and the calculation took months.

If Rubin was hoping to produce a conclusion that would not startle or upset people, she failed. The big-bang theory predicted that galaxies would be evenly distributed throughout the universe. Rubin's calculation, however, showed that the universe seemed to be "lumpy." There were more galaxies in some parts than others. It was to be 15 years before other scientists proved Rubin right. The finding of a lumpy universe has made astronomers rethink their ideas about what happened during the big bang. They are still trying to figure out what the lumpiness means.

Rubin got her Ph.D. in 1954. She then taught and did research at Georgetown, in addition to caring for a growing family that included Karl (born 1956) and Allan (born 1960).

The place Rubin really wanted to work, however, was a small research laboratory called the Department of Terrestrial Magnetism. The DTM, as it was known, was part of the Carnegie Institution of Washington. Its original purpose had been to map the earth's magnetic field. Later, however, the DTM supported scientists who worked on many projects.

Rubin had first visited the DTM when she was a graduate student at Georgetown. "I . . . liked the way the place worked, and I liked the people. . . . I decided then that that was the place I would like to work," she says. "I . . . waited until I thought they would hire me, and then I walked in and asked for a job." In 1965 she got it. She still works there—and still loves it.

One reason why Rubin wanted to work at the DTM was that an astronomer named Kent Ford worked there. Ford had just built a new kind of spectrograph that could gather light 10 times faster than the old ones. Using Ford's spectrograph, which had an added device called an image tube, Rubin could photograph a galaxy's spectrum in 3 hours instead of 30.

Around 1970 Rubin turned Ford's spectrograph toward Andromeda, the closest galaxy visible from the Northern Hemisphere. Like most galaxies, Andromeda is shaped like a pinwheel. It has a flat disk with a bright, bulging center packed with stars.

Vera Rubin measuring galaxy spectra. The microscope-like machine allows Rubin to detect small differences in the spectra. These differences or shifts tell her how fast different parts of galaxies are rotating.
(Courtesy Carnegie Institution of Washington)

Arms curve out from the galaxy's center in a spiral pattern. Rubin wanted to compare the movements of the stars near the center with the movement of stars in the galaxy's outer parts.

Stars rotate around a galaxy's center much as the planets in our solar system rotate around the sun. Andromeda's disk is tilted at an angle toward the earth. This means that, at any given time, the stars on one side of Andromeda will be moving toward the earth and those on the other side will be moving away, as compared to Andromeda's center. The spectra of the stars moving toward the earth will therefore show blue shifts, while those moving away will show red shifts. By looking at spectra through a microscope, Rubin could measure the small shifts in their lines. The size of the shifts told her how fast each part of the galaxy turned.

Most of a galaxy's light is in its center. Rubin, like everyone else at the time, assumed that most of the mass or matter in a galaxy would also be in its center. If this was the case, Isaac Newton's laws of gravity predicted that the stars near the outside of the galaxy should orbit the galaxy's center much more slowly than the stars near the center. These same laws explain why, for example, the planet Pluto, which is 100 times farther from our sun than Mercury, travels 10 times more slowly than Mercury. (Most of the mass in our solar system is also in the system's center—the sun.)

When Rubin and Ford analyzed their spectra of the different parts of Andromeda, however, they found that our sister galaxy was doing something very odd. The stars in Andromeda's outer parts were moving just as fast as those nearer the center. Unable to explain this result, the two astronomers set it aside. They assumed that the oddity was some special feature of Andromeda.

Rubin and Ford then returned to the puzzling discovery Rubin had made while doing her master's thesis: that large groups of galaxies showed a motion in addition to that explained by the expanding universe. They confirmed this finding, using more galaxies and more exact measurements than had been possible before. The large-scale motion became known as the Rubin-Ford effect. Many astronomers still had trouble believing it, but later research has supported it. Nearly all studies now show large areas in space where galaxies move together toward regions of higher density. Astronomers assume that gravity causes this motion.

In the mid-1970s Rubin and Ford went back to the Andromeda mystery. They began measuring the speed of star rotation in other bright, nearby galaxies to see whether these would show the same strange behavior as Andromeda. Here again Ford's special spectrograph was a great help. Most distant galaxies appear as single dots of light even through a telescope. Relatively nearby galaxies, however, cover a small region of the sky. Ford's spectrograph had a long slit that could take advantage of this extended size and make different spectra for different parts of a galaxy.

After studying the spectra for each galaxy, Rubin and Ford plotted rotational velocity (speed of rotation) against distance from the galaxy's center. The result was a graph called a rotation curve. All the galaxies the two astronomers looked at showed rotation curves much like Andromeda's. Rotational velocity went up, not down, as distance from the galactic center grew. It quickly

The Andromeda galaxy. Vera Rubin's measurements of this nearby galaxy's rotation offered one of the first hints that most of the matter in the universe is invisible.
(Courtesy Yerkes Observatory)

reached a plateau, which stayed the same all the way out to what looked like the edge of the galaxy. Sometimes the stars and gas in the outer part of the galaxy were rotating even faster than those in the inner part.

Rubin herself did not recognize the importance of what she was seeing at first. "It took getting many [spectra] . . . over a couple of nights, to realize that they all looked very much the same and all rather surprising."

"Rather surprising," indeed! The stars in the outer parts of the galaxies were moving so fast that they ought to be escaping the galaxy's gravity and flying off in all directions. That was not happening. This meant that one of two things had to be true: either Newton's laws broke down over such a large scale, or there was a large amount of mass in the galaxies that no one could see. The gravitational attraction of this extra mass could cause the stars to orbit the galaxy more quickly than expected.

There was no reason to doubt Newton's laws, so Rubin was left with an equally startling conclusion: "The distribution of mass within a galaxy was not at all like the distribution of light." Each galaxy seemed to be surrounded by a sphere of invisible matter that extended well beyond the edge of the galaxy's visible disk.

Vera Rubin was not the first to suggest that a large part of the universe might be made up of something we can't see. In the 1930s two astronomers, Fritz Zwicky and Sinclair Smith, had proposed the same thing. They based their ideas on measurements of a cluster of galaxies. Like the stars and gas that Rubin measured, these galaxies proved to be moving too fast to stay together unless they were held by the gravity of what Zwicky called "missing mass." At the time, however, most other astronomers did not accept Zwicky's ideas.

Rubin and Ford eventually made rotation curves for about 200 galaxies. The curves all show the same thing. Along with other evidence, they have forced most astronomers to accept the existence of what is now called "dark matter." (As the name change suggests, astronomers have realized that the mass is not really missing. They just can't see it.)

What is the invisible matter that seems to make up 90 percent of the universe? No one knows. It may be small, dim stars or planets the size of Jupiter. Or it may be, as Rubin says, "something so different that we haven't even really imagined it yet." Rubin herself offers no suggestions about the dark matter's identity. Like Chien-shiung Wu, she prefers to concentrate on what she can observe and leave theorizing to others.

Vera Rubin has now reached an age at which many people think of retiring, but she has no such plans. "None whatsoever!" she says firmly. If she were not working, she claims, she would "weep again" as she did when her career seemed to be dissolving into diapers and playground trips.

Rubin is one of only 75 women members (out of a total of about 3,500) of the prestigious National Academy of Sciences. She serves on the Academy's Committee on Human Rights. Like Jewel Cobb, she has worked on programs that teach science to inner city students. Rubin's advice to young women interested in science is "to absolutely not give up, . . . not let anyone discourage them." Obviously, she has taken her own advice.

Chronology

July 23, 1928	Vera Cooper born in Philadelphia
1938	Cooper family moves to Washington, D.C.; Vera begins watching the stars
1948	Vera Cooper graduates from Vassar, marries Bob Rubin, attends Cornell
1950	Vera Rubin presents master's thesis paper on rotation of galaxies
1951	receives master's degree from Cornell
1954	receives Ph.D. from Georgetown University for thesis on uneven distribution of galaxies; begins research and teaching at Georgetown
1965	begins work at Department of Terrestrial Magnetism
1970	finds stars in outer part of Andromeda galaxy rotating faster than expected
early 1970s	discovers Rubin-Ford effect
mid-1970s to mid-1980s	measures rotation of stars in galaxies and demonstrates that up to 90 percent of universe is made of dark, unknown matter

Further Reading

Bartusiak, Marcia. "The Woman Who Spins the Stars." *Discover,* October 1990. Excellent description of Rubin's life, personality, and work.

Gleasner, Diana C. *Breakthrough: Women in Science.* New York: Walker & Co., 1983. For young adults. Chapter on Rubin deals mainly with her personal life and how she overcame difficulties.

Lightman, Alan, and Roberta Brawer. *Origins: The Lives and Worlds of Modern Cosmologists.* Cambridge: Harvard University Press, 1990. Includes a long interview with Vera Rubin.

Overbye, Dennis. *Lonely Hearts of the Cosmos.* New York: Harper & Row, 1992. Only a small part of this book deals with Rubin, but the book places her work in the context of other recent astronomical discoveries and gives an interesting picture of the way astronomers work.

Rubin, Vera C. "Dark Matter in Spiral Galaxies." *Scientific American,* June 1983. Describes Rubin's most important discovery. Difficult reading.

———. "Galactic Go-Around." *Natural History,* August 1980. Provides background on galaxies and their movements and gives reasons for thinking that most matter in galaxies is dark.

———. "Stars, Galaxies, Cosmos: The Past Decade, The Next Decade." *Science,* July 4, 1980. Describes discoveries during the 1970s, including the discovery of dark matter, that changed the way astronomers view the universe; also speculates on discoveries that might be made in the 1980s. Difficult reading.

———. "Women's Work." *Science 86,* July–August 1986. Interesting article by Rubin describes the work of Maria Mitchell, Annie Jump Cannon, and other women astronomers of earlier times.

Candace Beebe Pert
(1946–)

Candace Beebe Pert. Pert's study of brain chemicals and
their receptors has given important information about how
the brain works and how mind and body
may communicate.
(Courtesy Candace Pert)

*O*ne day in the 21st century, a man shows signs of mental illness.
His family takes him to a doctor. The doctor orders a scan of the
man's brain. The scan shows which of the brain's complex chemical systems is malfunctioning and how. The doctor then pre-
scribes medications that restore the man to normal. These drugs
compare to today's drug treatments for mental illness as a
surgeon's scalpel compares to an axe.

Elsewhere in the same future city, a woman learns that she has cancer. The disease is advanced, and she is in pain. Yet her doctor does not order surgery or toxic drugs. Instead, the doctor directs the woman to a clinic. There she learns how to use deep breathing to release natural pain-killing chemicals in her brain. She also learns how to strengthen and direct her immune system cells in their battle against the invading disease.

If either or both of these medical dreams become real, Candace Pert—or her spirit—will be able to say "I told you so." Beginning while she was still a graduate student, Pert has been a leader in studying the complex chemistry of the brain. She has helped to show that the mind and the body are linked more closely than anyone dreamed. Indeed, she says, "It's all one thing"—what she calls the "bodymind."

Candace Dorinda Beebe was born in New York City on June 26, 1946. She grew up in Wantagh, Long Island. Her father, Robert, held jobs ranging from selling radio advertising to arranging band music. Mildred, her mother, worked part time as a court clerk. William Beebe, an underwater explorer who was Eugenie Clark's childhood hero, was a relative of Candace's.

Candace didn't major in science when she went to Hofstra University, near her home. "My goal in life was to be an editor of *Mademoiselle* magazine," she has said. Her interests began to change, however, when she met a blond Estonian named Agu Pert. Agu was a graduate student in psychology. He and Candace spent some of their dates cleaning out animal cages in the psychology lab. They also talked about science. Candace found she liked science's precision and objectivity.

Candace and Agu Pert were married in March 1966, before Candace completed her bachelor's degree. Their first child, Evan, was born soon after. Agu went on to further studies at Bryn Mawr, a college near Philadelphia, while Candace stayed home to take care of the baby. Like Vera Rubin, she found herself miserable as a full-time housewife. She signed up at Bryn Mawr to finish her degree, this time as a science major.

Agu Pert had to do military service in Maryland, so Candace looked for a place nearby to do her graduate studies. She chose Johns Hopkins Medical School in Baltimore (where Helen Taussig still practiced) because she had heard about a scientist there named Solomon Snyder. Snyder was studying a subject that interested Pert but attracted few others at the time: the chemistry of the brain. Pert shares an interest in body chemistry with Gertrude Elion and Flossie Wong-Staal.

Pert joined Snyder's lab in the fall of 1970. She was bored with the first research project he gave her. She wanted to work on something new and exciting. Snyder liked to break new ground, too. They finally agreed on a project: Pert would try to find the opiate receptor.

Since at least 1905, scientists had assumed that drugs must attach to "receptive substances" in the body before they could act. No one, however, had been able to find such substances. Then, in the late 1960s, scientists showed that molecules of a few body chemicals, such as insulin (which controls blood sugar), could attach or bind to tissues they were known to affect. It seemed likely that the chemicals were sticking to receptor molecules in the tissues. These binding experiments gave the first direct evidence that receptors were real. Scientists began to look for more receptors. As Pert says, "receptors were in the air."

Concern about opiates and other addictive drugs was also in the air. Opiates include opium, morphine, and heroin. Some reports said that one of every four American soldiers in the Vietnam War was addicted to heroin. Opiate drugs were also linked to growing crime in cities. In 1971 President Nixon declared a "war on drugs." Finding a receptor for opiates might help doctors fight drug addiction.

It might seem strange to think the body would have receptors for substances that most people never encounter. Still, Snyder and Pert had reasons to think opiate receptors existed. One reason was the fact that certain chemicals are almost exactly like the opiates, yet have little or no effect on the body. Molecules of these chemicals are mirror images of opiate molecules. Maria Mayer and Chien-shiung Wu had shown that "handedness" makes a difference in the behavior of subatomic particles. It makes a difference for many molecules, too. Just as a right hand will not fit a left-hand glove, a "right-handed" molecule would not fit a left-handed receptor. Snyder and Pert believed the mirror-image drugs were inactive because they did not fit the opiate receptors.

In 1971 a scientist named Avram Goldstein had tried to find opiate receptors and failed. Snyder and Pert read about his work. Around the beginning of 1972, Snyder suggested that Pert try to improve on Goldstein's experiments.

Following Goldstein's lead, Pert worked with an opiate solution that had been "tagged" with radioactive atoms. She poured this solution over ground-up rat brain. She washed and filtered the tissue, then measured the radioactivity left in it. This showed how much drug had stuck to the tissue.

Both drugs and natural substances can cling to tissue in many ways. Most of these ways have nothing to do with receptors. They are called nonspecific binding. Pert had to find a way to show how much of the binding she detected was nonspecific and how much was specific, or due to receptors.

Goldstein had tried to do this by comparing the binding of an active opiate with that of an inactive, "mirror-image" opiate. The active opiate could bind both specifically and nonspecifically. The inactive opiate, however, could bind only nonspecifically. The difference in radiation count for the two substances therefore should show the amount of specific binding.

The trouble was that Goldstein had found almost no difference—just 2 percent. During the summer of 1972, Pert tried many versions of Goldstein's technique. None produced any better results. (Pert learned later that the opiate she had been using failed to work because it broke down under light.)

Snyder began to be afraid that Pert was wasting her time. He suggested that she drop the project. Pert refused. "It took a lot of faith and stick-to-it-iveness," she says. "[But] the evidence was, in my mind, overwhelming that these receptors should be there, if I could just find the right conditions. . . . Then one day, bang, the magic conditions came up."

One of the magic conditions proved to be using naloxone instead of an opiate in the tests. Naloxone canceled opiates' effects, probably by pushing opiate molecules off receptors. It was used to revive people who had taken heroin overdoses.

Pert tried naloxone on September 22, 1972. When she saw her results, she took them straight to Snyder's office. "Look at this," she said. "You're not going to believe it."

Snyder read the numbers and let out a howl of joy. Sixty-six percent of the binding was specific!

For the next few months Pert spent 11-hour days in the lab. She repeated her experiments many times. She also tested different opiates to see how well they competed with naloxone for receptor binding. Pert found that the more effective an opiate was as a drug, the better it competed with naloxone. She also found that nonopiate drugs did not compete with naloxone. Furthermore, naloxone

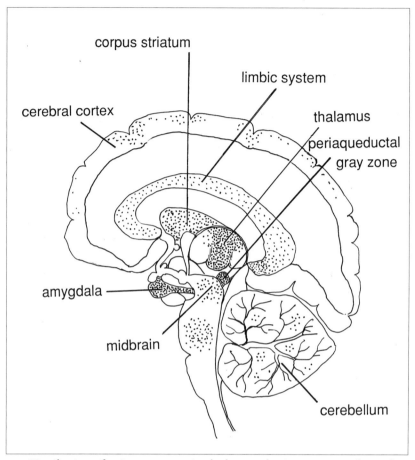

corpus striatum

limbic system

cerebral cortex

thalamus

periaqueductal gray zone

amygdala

midbrain

cerebellum

Distribution of opiate receptors in the human brain. Large numbers of receptors have been found in the periaqueductal gray area, which is involved in pain perception, and in the limbic system, which is involved in pleasure and other emotions.
(Courtesy Katherine MacFarlane)

binding was strongest in parts of the brain known to be involved in the perception of pain. This made sense, because opiates acted as painkillers. All these results suggested that the naloxone was really binding to opiate receptors.

Pert and Snyder published a paper describing Pert's experiments. It appeared in *Science,* America's most important general-purpose scientific journal, on March 9, 1973. Johns Hopkins also held a press conference to announce the discovery. Newspaper, magazine, and TV reporters came. At age 26, Candace Pert suddenly found herself famous.

Hopes that the discovery raised at the time did not come true. Finding the opiate receptor did not lead to a cure for drug addiction. It did not lead to development of a nonaddictive drug that could control pain. Still, Pert's work was very important. It provided a technique for finding all kinds of receptors. It also offered a simple way to screen drugs for effectiveness. Pert's discovery was the first receptor found in the brain and the first receptor for a compound that did not exist naturally in the body.

Scientists in Snyder's lab and elsewhere now began trying to answer an obvious question: Why were the opiate receptors there? The receptors surely must respond to an unknown natural brain substance that was like opium. Hans Kosterlitz and John Hughes at the University of Aberdeen, Scotland, were the first to find such a substance. On December 18, 1975, they announced the discovery of a compound that they called enkephalin. Enkephalin proved to be one of a group of chemicals that were later named the endorphins. The name is short for "endogenous [naturally occurring within the body] morphinelike compounds."

Candace Pert, meanwhile, continued to study opiate—or rather endorphin—receptors. She had won her Ph.D. in 1974 but stayed on for an extra year at Johns Hopkins. Working in the laboratory of Michael Kuhar, Pert invented a way to show exactly where these receptors were in the brain. She injected a powerful radioactive opiate into rats. Then she killed the animals and cut their brains into slices. She exposed each slice to photographic film. Radioactive material causes silver grains on film to develop. Making photos by exposing film to radioactivity is called autoradiography.

The radioactively marked receptors in the photographed brain slices glowed like clusters of stars in a night sky. The brighter the glow, the thicker the receptors were. Pert's photos made a map of the brain's opiate receptors. Later, as receptors for other brain chemicals were discovered, Pert's technique was used to make maps for these receptors as well.

Pert found that large numbers of opiate receptors "lit up" parts of the brain involved in pain perception. More surprisingly, an area called the limbic system also blazed with receptors. Rats allowed to stimulate their limbic systems electrically by pushing a bar would do so until they dropped from exhaustion. This area thus seemed to be a center for feelings of pleasure. Activity of opiates in the limbic system could explain the pleasurable "rush" that makes opiate addicts crave their drug. More important, finding opiate receptors in this area suggested that endorphins are the body's natural pleasure chemicals. The brain releases them to

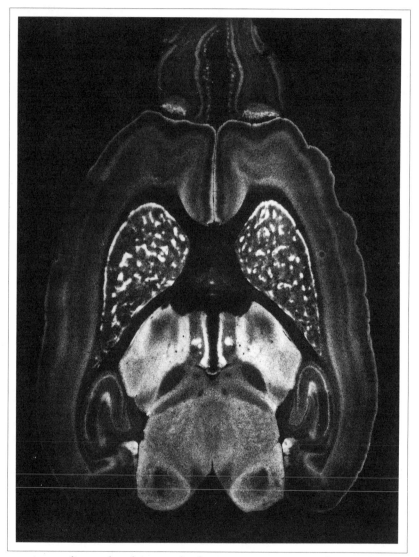

Autoradiography photograph of opiate receptors in rat brain. The bright areas, marked by a radioactive opiate, show large numbers of receptors.
(Courtesy Miles Herkenham, NIMH)

reward actions that help an individual or a species survive, such as eating, mating, and caring for young.

In September 1975 Candace and Agu Pert both got jobs at the National Institute of Mental Health (NIMH). This is one of the National Institutes of Health, a group of large, government-sponsored research institutions in Bethesda, Maryland. (Flossie Wong-Staal was studying cancer viruses in another one of these institutions when the Perts arrived.) Unusually for one so young, Candace Pert became head of her own lab. She soon had students of her own. She also had a new daughter, Vanessa. Pert continued her work on receptor mapping at NIMH. She also looked for, and in some cases found, new receptors for both natural chemicals and drugs.

Pert found herself famous again in the fall of 1978. Solomon Snyder, Hans Kosterlitz, and John Hughes won an important science prize called the Lasker Award. When Pert heard the news, she wrote a letter to Mary Lasker, the prize's sponsor. "I was angry and upset to be excluded from this year's award," Pert's letter said. "As Dr. Snyder's graduate student, I played a key role in initiating the [opiate receptor] research and following it up." Copies of Pert's letter found their way to magazines that covered news about science, and women reporters at two of the magazines wrote stories about it. They suggested that Pert had failed to receive the Lasker award because she was a woman.

The award committee never explained their decision. Scientists were divided about its fairness. Some thought Pert and the reporters were right. Others assumed that Pert had not gotten the award because she had been a graduate student when she did the work on the opiate receptor. Although Hughes was also young, he already had his Ph.D. Many scientists blamed Pert for making her feelings public.

Today, Pert simply says that it was all "a long time ago now" and she is sick of talking about the matter. But she adds, "I have no regrets whatsoever that I spoke up. I think it was a good thing to do."

As the "Lasker flap" died down, Pert went on with her personal and professional life. In 1978 she won the Arthur S. Fleming Award for outstanding government service. She had a third child, Brandon, in 1982. In 1983 she became chief of a new section on brain biochemistry in the Clinical Neuroscience Branch of NIMH. She was the only woman section chief in the institute at the time.

Pert continued to look for new brain chemicals and their receptors. She and other scientists noticed that many of these chemicals were simple substances called peptides. Peptides are short chains of amino acids. (Longer chains of amino acids are called proteins.) The endorphins are peptides, as are many hormones, such as insulin. During the early 1980s Pert realized that her "life's work" would be the study of these message-carrying peptides and their receptors.

Today about 70 messenger peptides are known. They are sometimes called neuropeptides because they are found in the brain. They also appear in the intestine, the immune system, and other parts of the body. They help to regulate digestion, sexual activity, blood pressure, and many other body functions. They have been found in almost all forms of life, from humans to one-celled animals. Pert feels that the neuropeptides and their receptors form a system or network for communication between cells. Cells use these compounds to send messages to other cells far away in the body. Only cells with the right receptors will receive the messages.

In the early 1980s Pert and her coworkers, as well as scientists in other laboratories, began to find evidence that neuropeptides and their receptors linked the brain and the immune system. (The immune system defends the body against disease.) The scientists found receptors for these brain chemicals on immune system cells. The peptides changed the speed and direction of the cells' movement. Some of the cells could also make neuropeptides. Pert discovered that certain receptors first found on immune system cells existed in the brain as well.

"One of the things about research [is that] you never know where things are going to lead," Pert says. That was certainly true of her immune system research. Around 1984 she discovered certain immune cell receptors, called CD-4 receptors, in the brain. Soon afterward she heard that the virus that causes AIDS (which Flossie Wong-Staal had helped to discover the year before) uses these same receptors to enter cells. "We said, 'Wow, this is important,'" Pert recalls. "That led to the idea that we could invent a drug that would block those receptors." Such a drug might stop AIDS in its tracks.

Candace Pert had never intended to go into AIDS research. Her drug idea, however, seemed too good not to follow up. Another NIMH scientist named Michael Ruff worked with her. Candace had been divorced from Agu Pert in 1982, and she and Ruff became close. They were married in 1986.

The drug they developed is called Peptide T. It is similar to the part of the virus envelope that binds to the CD-4 receptor. Pert and Ruff began publishing papers about Peptide T in 1986. They claimed that it blocked AIDS virus reproduction effectively in the test tube. Some other scientists said they had trouble reproducing Pert's results, however. Pert believes this is because "they. . . used everything different—different viruses, different concentrations of viruses." She also states that these scientists were consultants for companies that were developing competing AIDS drugs.

Pert and Ruff felt that "the government wasn't taking [Peptide T] seriously" for political reasons. They therefore left NIMH at the end of 1987 to develop the drug on their own. They found supporting investors and set up a company called Peptide Design. A large drug company bought a license to make Peptide T, but a few years later it withdrew its support. At that point, Pert says, "all the investors lost heart," and Peptide Design "crashed and burned." Pert and Ruff refused to give up, however. Later they found new investors and continued their work.

Pert still believes that Peptide T will be an effective AIDS drug. She feels it is her most important scientific discovery so far. "We stand by our original results," she says firmly. The compound is now being tested on people.

Pert's main interest today is the linkage between the mind and the body. A new science with a jawbreaking name, psychoneuroimmunology, has been created to study these links. Pert's research with peptides and their receptors has helped to show a means by which mind and body can communicate.

Pert and others in this new field believe that feelings may affect the way the body resists disease. A person who is constantly unhappy or tense might get sick more easily than someone who is not. An optimistic person might be better able to fight off illness than a pessimistic one. Some research has supported these ideas. Links between emotions and immunity, however, remain complex and mysterious.

Someday, if scientists decode all the neuropeptides' messages, doctors may treat many illnesses with drugs that change the amount of neuropeptides or receptors. But an opposite approach might work equally well. "Sure, our minds are chemicals. Everything is chemistry," Pert says. "But I think it's a big, big mistake to say that leads to drugs and more drugs. . . . I think what we're talking about is understanding ourselves." She believes that people in the future will be able to heal most illnesses by calling on the "drugstores" in their own bodies.

One way of measuring a scientist's importance is by counting how many times other scientists cite or refer to the scientist's papers when writing about their own work. Important papers influence many people and thus are cited often. A study by the Institute for Scientific Information in Philadelphia named Pert as one of the 10 women scientists whose work was cited most often during the 1980s. One science reporter says Pert's paper on the opiate receptor is "one of the most cited research papers in all of modern biology." Pert also has won recent awards, such as the Kilby Award in 1993.

But Pert is memorable for reasons besides her work. Like many strong and colorful women, she produces powerful reactions in those who know her. Frederick Goodwin, former head of the Alcohol, Drug Abuse, and Mental Health Administration, says, "Candace has one of the most inventive and creative minds I know of in neuroscience." Another admirer says, "[Her] energy and optimism . . . explode like a Roman candle." But other scientists complain that Pert makes strong statements she cannot always support. "She's superb. A very bright mind," says Edith Hendley, a scientist who has worked with her. "But she has an inability to edit herself. . . . She does crazy things without thinking them out. Of course," Hendley adds, "they're very interesting things."

Candace Pert says emphatically that she "detests" controversy. Unlike Vera Rubin, however, Pert seldom goes out of her way to avoid it. A card on Pert's wall says, "If you are getting run out of town, get in front of the crowd and make it look like a parade." Pert knows how to lead a parade.

Pert believes that "in science you are uncovering eternal truth." She adds, "If it's the truth and you believe in it, then you . . . have a responsibility to take it as far as it needs to go." Candace Pert has always been willing to take her ideas as far as they will go. Perhaps not all of those ideas will prove to be right. But some of them may make a change—perhaps a major change—in the way we treat illness and understand ourselves.

Chronology

June 26, 1946	Candace Dorinda Beebe born in New York City
1966	marries Agu Pert
fall 1970	enters Solomon Snyder's laboratory at Johns Hopkins Medical School
September 22, 1972	discovers opiate receptors
March 9, 1973	paper on opiate receptors published in *Science*
1974	receives Ph.D. from Johns Hopkins
1975	develops autoradiography method for mapping receptors in brain; moves to National Institutes of Mental Health; enkephalin discovered
1978	protests exclusion from Lasker Award; wins Arthur S. Fleming Award
1982	divorced from Agu Pert
1983	becomes chief of brain biochemistry section at NIMH
1984	discovers CD-4 receptors in brain
1986	begins publishing papers on Peptide T; marries Michael Ruff
1987	leaves NIMH to develop Peptide T
1990	Peptide Design fails
1993	wins Kilby Award
1980s–present	does research on psychoneuroimmunology

Further Reading

Arehart-Treichel, Joan. "Winning and Losing: The Medical Awards Game." *Science News*, February 14, 1979. This account of the Lasker Award controversy maintains that Pert was denied the award because she was a woman.

Barnes, Deborah M. "Debate over Potential AIDS Drug." *Science*, July 10, 1987. Describes conflicting views of effectiveness of Peptide T.

Goldberg, Jeff. *Anatomy of a Scientific Discovery.* New York: Bantam, 1988. Describes the discovery of opiate receptors and the search for natural opiatelike chemicals.

Goldberg, Joan. "Peptide Power." *American Health,* June 1990. Summarizes Pert's recent career and her ideas about the importance of peptides in the body.

Hall, Stephen S. "A Molecular Code Links Emotions, Mind and Health." *Smithsonian,* June 1989. Describes discoveries in the infant field of psychoneuroimmunology, including those of Pert.

Kanigel, Robert. *Apprentice to Genius.* New York: Macmillan, 1986. Portrays a group of scientists, including Snyder and Pert, who have changed science's view of the brain; provides the fullest account of Pert's early work.

Pert, Candace. "The Material Basis of Emotions." *Whole Earth Review,* Summer 1988. Pert explains some of her discoveries about peptides and their implications for medicine and health.

——— and Solomon H. Snyder. "Opiate Receptor: Demonstration in Nervous Tissue." *Science,* March 9, 1973. The original paper describing Pert's isolation of the opiate receptor. Difficult reading.

Weintraub, Pamela, ed. *The Omni Interviews.* New York: Omni Press/Ticknor and Fields, 1984. Includes a 1981 interview with Pert that focuses on her ideas about brain mapping and the link between emotions and brain chemistry.

Flossie Wong-Staal
(1946–)

Flossie Wong-Staal. Wong-Staal has analyzed the genes of the virus that causes AIDS and is now looking for a cure for this deadly disease.
(Courtesy Flossie Wong-Staal)

At first, around 1981, it was just a cluster of symptoms (signs of illness) that showed up among people, mostly homosexual men, in a few cities. They became weak and lost weight. Some came down with a rare form of pneumonia (a lung disease). Some got purple blotches on their skins, the mark of an unusual cancer. Then, one by one, they began to die.

A few puzzled doctors wrote scientific papers about the strange syndrome (group of symptoms). They were not even sure that they were describing a single disease. If it was a disease, it seemed to be new to science.

Then more cases began to appear. Some of the sick people had lived in or visited Haiti or certain other Caribbean countries. Some were drug abusers. Some simply had had blood transfusions.

By 1983 the collection of symptoms had a name: acquired immune deficiency syndrome, or AIDS. The name reflected the one feature that all the sick people had in common, an immune system that could no longer protect the body effectively. People with AIDS usually died from illnesses caused by microbes that did not harm healthy people. Underlying these illnesses, most doctors came to agree, was a single disease that destroyed the immune system. But no one knew what caused the disease.

In late 1983 research laboratories in the United States and France showed that the cause of AIDS was a virus. The virus was later given the name of HIV, short for human immunodeficiency virus. Medical researchers all over the world have studied HIV intensely since then. Some hope to make a vaccine to protect people against the virus. Others seek treatments for those who are already infected.

If this work succeeds, it will owe much to Flossie Wong-Staal. Wong-Staal has been part of the fight against AIDS from the beginning. She worked in the American laboratory that helped to identify the AIDS virus. She has learned more about the virus than almost anyone else. Today she is contributing to the searches for both a vaccine and a cure for AIDS. She has also done important research on the causes of cancer, which kills far more people than AIDS.

Flossie Wong-Staal was born in Kuangchou (which English-speakers called Canton), in southern China, on August 27, 1946. Her name then was Yee-ching Wong. Her father, Sueh-fung Wong, was a businessman who imported and exported cloth. The Wongs had two daughters and a son (another son came along later), and Yee-ching was the younger daughter.

A Communist government took control of China in 1949. Sueh-fung Wong was visiting Hong Kong, a small British colony on the south China coast, at the time of the takeover. For some time he could not contact his family. Then, after many petitions to the government, his wife, Wei-chung, and their children were allowed to leave China in 1952. The Wongs set up a new home in the city of Hong Kong.

Yee-ching got a new name when she went to school. The English-speaking teachers told her father that she ought to have an English name. Then they handed him a sheet with the names of all the typhoons that had struck Hong Kong! These fierce tropical storms, similar to hurricanes, used to be given English women's names. Yee-ching's father picked the name Flossie from the sheet.

Flossie's high school, like others in Hong Kong, assigned students to either liberal arts or science. Flossie, like Chien-shiung Wu many years before her, was told that she was going to be a science major. She saw being chosen for science as a privilege, and she enjoyed her science classes.

Many students in Hong Kong chose to go to college in the United States. Flossie Wong picked the University of California at Los Angeles (UCLA) because several of her friends were going there. She entered UCLA in 1965.

In her later undergraduate years Flossie Wong took courses in molecular biology. This is the study of the structure and function of chemicals in the bodies of living things. This field was as thrilling in the late 1960s as nuclear physics had been in the 1920s for Maria Mayer and in the 1930s for Chien-shiung Wu. Scientists had learned how to read the chemical code in which the genes (units of information on DNA molecules) carry inherited information, and they were just beginning to learn how to change genes. "It was a very exciting time, and I was just fascinated by it," Wong-Staal remembers. She shares this fascination with the chemistry of life with Gertrude Elion and Candace Pert.

Flossie Wong married a fellow biology major named Steven Staal in 1971 and changed her name to the combined form Wong-Staal. The newlyweds had to make a hundred-mile commute to be together, because Flossie was studying for her Ph.D. at UCLA and Steven was in medical school at the University of California in San Diego. Wong-Staal got her degree in 1972. She was named Outstanding Woman Graduate of the Year. She also gave birth to a daughter, Stephanie.

The war in Vietnam was reaching its peak in the early 1970s. Steven Staal chose to do civilian work for the government instead of fighting in the war. He was assigned to the National Institutes of Health (NIH), the huge cluster of government research institutes in Bethesda, Maryland. Flossie Wong-Staal arranged to work there as well. She joined Robert Gallo's laboratory at NIH in 1973. (Candace Pert, who had just discovered the opiate receptor, would come to a different part of NIH two years later.)

Gallo's main project at the time was studying the genes of viruses that caused cancer in animals. Thus Flossie Wong-Staal, like Jewel Cobb, began to do research on cancer. Viruses, so tiny that they can be seen only with an electron microscope, hover on the border between living and nonliving things. They consist of genetic information (nucleic acid) wrapped in a protein coat or envelope. They can reproduce only by entering a living cell. They insert their genetic material into that of the cell, then use the cell's chemical machinery to make copies of themselves.

Around the time Wong-Staal entered Gallo's lab, scientists began to discover that some viruses could cause cancer in animals by turning on special genes called oncogenes. Normally these genes regulate cell growth. They are active only at certain times. If they become turned on all the time, they cause cells to grow uncontrollably. When some cancer-causing viruses reproduce, they turn on oncogenes that are already in the cell. In other cases, the viruses introduce oncogenes as part of their own genetic information. Scientists found that these oncogenes came from cells that the viruses had infected earlier. In other words, all "virus" oncogenes are really cell oncogenes.

Some animal cancer viruses are DNA viruses. Their genetic information, like that of the cells they infect, is carried in molecules of DNA (deoxyribonucleic acid). To make proteins, viruses and cells alike translate their DNA information into the form of another nucleic acid, RNA (ribonucleic acid).

In the late 1960s, however, scientists discovered a group of viruses that work differently. They carry their genetic information in the form of RNA, then translate it into DNA in cells. To do this they use a chemical called reverse transcriptase. Because these RNA viruses work backward compared to other viruses and cells, they came to be called retroviruses (retro- means backward).

Some retroviruses also cause cancer in animals. One common one produces leukemia in cats. Others cause cancers in monkeys and apes, humans' closest animal relatives. Robert Gallo believed that retroviruses might also cause cancer in people. Few other researchers shared his belief at that time.

Flossie Wong-Staal studied monkey and ape cancer retroviruses during her first years in Gallo's lab. Along with others at the lab, she picked out oncogenes, or what might be oncogenes, in the viruses. Then she tried to find genes in human cells that matched or were similar to them. Her group was among the first to find genes in human cells that matched these retrovirus oncogenes. Wong-Staal's work added to scientists' recognition that oncogenes were normal cell genes that certain viruses had picked up.

Gallo was impressed with Wong-Staal's work from the beginning. He wrote later that she "evolve[d] into one of the major players in my group. Because of her insight and leadership qualities, she gradually assumed a supervisory role." She, in turn, says, "that laboratory has made more original discoveries than any lab I know in biomedical science." She and Gallo clearly made a good team. "He's . . . creative and goes after original observations . . . while my interest was more analytical," Wong-Staal says. In this practical bent she is like Chien-shiung Wu and Vera Rubin.

During the 1970s Gallo, Wong-Staal, and others in Gallo's lab pursued their search for a retrovirus that could cause cancer in humans. They worked out tests that could identify reverse transcriptase in cells. They found this chemical in some human cancer cells. Finally, in 1981, they isolated a retrovirus from certain human leukemia cells. They offered good evidence that the virus caused the cancer.

Gallo called the new virus HTLV, for human T-cell leukemia virus. T cells are one kind of immune system cell in the blood. HTLV attacks only a certain kind of T cell. A protein on the virus coat attaches itself to a molecule, called a CD-4 receptor, on the surface of one of these cells. The virus then injects its genetic material into the cell. Candace Pert also found CD-4 receptors on brain cells.

Scientists found leukemia patients infected with HTLV in several parts of the world, including Japan and the Caribbean. They showed that the virus could be spread by sexual contact, by blood (transfusions, for example), and from mother to unborn child. Cancer arose many years after infection. Soon afterward Gallo's lab found a second, related cancer-causing retrovirus, which they called HTLV-2.

When reports about AIDS began to appear, Gallo and the others in his lab wondered immediately whether the strange syndrome might be caused by either HTLV-1 or a closely related virus. "I think what struck . . . us . . . is the mode of transmission—it seem[ed] very similar to the leukemia virus . . . and also the fact that it affects the immune system and that the specific cell that . . . disappears in AIDS is the . . . CD-4 [T] cell, . . . the cell that HTLV

111

transforms [makes cancerous]," Wong-Staal says. She notes that with some retroviruses that infect animals, such as the one that causes disease in cats, "the same virus . . . can induce a cell to grow uncontrollably . . . [or] kill it." Thus it seemed possible that a human leukemia virus could also cause AIDS, in which T cells are destroyed.

The lab soon found, however, that only about 10 percent of people with AIDS showed signs of infection by HTLVs. (These people proved to be infected with HTLVs as well as with the AIDS virus.) In many more patients Gallo's workers found signs of a virus that was not an HTLV. Their research and that of other labs suggested that this new virus would be like the HTLVs in some ways—similar enough that they gave it the name of HTLV-3—but different in others.

In late 1983, Gallo's lab isolated the virus. Luc Montagnier and other scientists at the Pasteur Institute in France isolated a similar virus, which they called LAV, at about the same time. The viruses turned out to be identical. The name of the virus was changed to HIV. The two labs later worked out blood tests that showed who had been exposed to the virus. All AIDS patients tested had signs of exposure.

Once the virus was isolated and purified, Flossie Wong-Staal applied her skills in molecular biology to analyzing it. In late 1984 she cloned the virus's genetic material, or made many copies of it, by growing it in bacteria. This made large amounts of the material available for study.

Wong-Staal and the researchers working under her then worked out the sequence of the virus's genetic material. HIV proved to have at least nine genes instead of the three that most other retroviruses have. "Working with this virus is like putting your hand in a treasure chest," Wong-Staal said. "Every time you put your hand in you pull out a gem."

Wong-Staal continued her painstaking work of analysis during the 1980s. She isolated each of the virus's genes and tried to find out what it did. She discovered that some or perhaps all of the virus's extra genes regulate the virus's growth. These genes are turned on at different times. They interact with each other and with the cell's genes in complicated ways. Understanding these regulatory genes helped to explain some of the mysteries of AIDS, such as why people often stayed well for up to a decade after being infected.

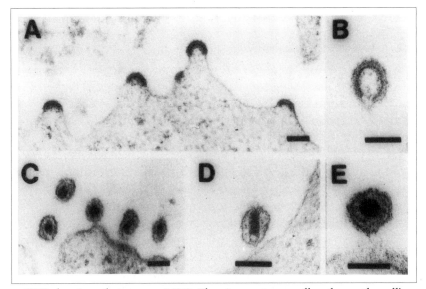

HIV, the virus that causes AIDS. The virus enters a cell and uses the cell's genetic machinery to make copies of itself. New virus particles then "bud" from the cell membrane, as shown here, and go on to infect other cells.
(Courtesy *Science* magazine, Vol. 225, 24 August 1984
[Copyright 1984 by American Association for the Advancement of Science],
and Jay A. Levy)

Wong-Staal and others also discovered that some parts of the virus's genetic information frequently change or mutate. Such changeability adds to the difficulty of making a vaccine. A vaccine makes the immune system prepare defenses against a particular microbe. If part of a microbe changes, a vaccine that protected the body against the original microbe may not be effective against the changed one.

Flossie Wong-Staal's own life changed around the end of the decade. Her marriage to Steven Staal ended in 1985. She now had to raise her two-year-old second daughter, Caroline, as a single mother. (Eugenie Clark, Jewel Cobb, and Candace Pert had faced similar challenges.) At the same time, AIDS research had become a "hot" field, and many universities offered her jobs. In 1990 Wong-Staal took over a new AIDS laboratory at the University of California at San Diego, the university that had been Maria

Mayer's last home. "It [was] always in the back of my mind that someday I want[ed] to come back to California," Wong-Staal says.

Although Wong-Staal continues to analyze the AIDS virus, she has concentrated in recent years on trying to develop vaccines and treatments for the disease. One possible vaccine is based on a part of the virus envelope called the V3 loop. Wong-Staal has created a sort of synthetic V3 octopus, a molecule with eight V3 "arms" attached to a central core. In animal tests, the octopus molecule produced an immune reaction 500 times stronger than that for the V3 loop alone. United Biomedical Inc. of Lake Success, New York, is now testing the V3 loop vaccine in humans.

Today Wong-Staal is turning her attention from vaccines to treatments, as Candace Pert did in the late 1980s with Peptide T. Wong-Staal has changed a chemical called a ribozyme so that it acts like a molecular knife or scissors. (The ribozyme came from a plant virus but has been modified to recognize HIV's genetic material.) The ribozyme cuts the virus's RNA apart and thus inactivates it. "We have very encouraging data that the ribozyme, if introduced in cells, can block infection as well as reproduction of the virus," Wong-Staal says. She warns that much more work must be done, however, before the treatment is ready for testing in humans. (The only widely accepted treatment for AIDS today is AZT, a drug developed in Gertrude Elion's Burroughs Wellcome lab.)

Flossie Wong-Staal, like Candace Pert, is only in her mid-forties but is already a highly respected scientist. Scientists usually cite or list at the end of their research papers the earlier papers that have influenced them. The more important a piece of research described in a paper, the more often that paper will be cited by other scientists. A computer study by the Institute of Scientific Information in Philadelphia found that Wong-Staal's papers were cited by other scientists more often than those of any other woman scientist in the 1980s. Her work was cited 7,772 times between 1981 and 1988.

Wong-Staal most likely will be active in biomedical research for decades to come. There is no way to know what she may achieve in that time. A vaccine or cure for AIDS? A basic discovery about how the immune system works? A key understanding of cancer or some other disease? With Wong-Staal's insight and persistence, anything seems possible.

Chronology

August 27, 1946	Yee-ching Wong born in Kuangchou, China
1952	moves with family to Hong Kong
1965	Flossie Wong enters UCLA
1971	marries Steven Staal
1972	gains Ph.D. from UCLA
1973	joins Robert Gallo's lab at National Institutes of Health
1981	Gallo's lab isolates first human cancer-causing retrovirus; first reports about AIDS appear
1983	Gallo's lab and French lab identify virus (HIV) that causes AIDS
1984	Wong-Staal clones genes of HIV
1985	divorced from Steven Staal
1985–89	analyzes HIV genes
1990	becomes head of AIDS lab at University of California at San Diego
1990–present	works on V3 loop and other AIDS vaccines and on ribozyme AIDS treatment

Further Reading

Baskin, Yvonne. "Intimate Enemies." *Discover,* December 1991. Biographical article about Wong-Staal and her discoveries, focusing on her most recent work.

Gallo, Robert. *Virus Hunting: AIDS, Cancer, and the Human Retrovirus.* New York: Basic Books, 1991. Describes the work of Gallo's laboratory in finding HTLV-1 and 2 and HIV; includes many mentions of Wong-Staal. Fairly difficult reading.

Haseltine, William A., and Flossie Wong-Staal. "The Molecular Biology of the AIDS Virus." *Scientific American,* October 1988. Describes the different genes of the AIDS virus and explains how they regulate virus growth. Difficult reading.

Index

Bold numbers indicate main headings.
Italic numbers indicate illustrations.

A

Acquired Immune Deficiency Syndrome—*See* AIDS
Actinomycin D 74
Acyclovir 54–55
Addiction, drug—*See* Drug addiction
AIDS 107–108, 111
  blood test 112
  drugs to treat 55, 102–103, 106, 114
  vaccine 113–114
  virus, discovery of 102, 108, 111–112, 116
Aiken, Howard 28, 29
Allopurinol 54
American Heart Association 9, 12
American Physical Society 45
Andromeda (galaxy) 87–89, *90*
Anemia, sickle-cell 44
Antimetabolites 50–51
Argonne National Laboratory 19, 25
Arthritis, rheumatoid 54
Astronomers, women 93
Atomic bomb 17–19, *18*, 28, 40
Atoms
  fission (splitting) 16–17
  nucleus 13–15, 17, 19–21, *22*, 25, 38–43—*See also* Radioactive breakdown of atoms; Shell theory
Autoradiography 99, *100*

Azathioprine 52–54
AZT 55, 114

B

Bases (of nucleic acids) 50–51, *51*, 55
Berkeley, University of California at—*See* California, University of—Berkeley
Beta decay (of atoms) 40–44—*See also* Radioactive breakdown of atoms
"Big bang" theory 85, 87
Binary number system 30
Birth defects
  heart 2–5
  thalidomide–caused 7–9, 12
Blalock, Alfred 5–7, 12
Blalock–Taussig operation 5–7, *6*, 12
Blood 3–4, 111
"Blue babies" 2–5
  operation to cure 5–7, *6*, 9–10, 12
Bohr, Niels 15, 16, 17, 20
Bomb, atomic—*See* Atomic bomb
Born, Max 14, 15, 16
Brain
  chemistry of 95–96, *98*, 99–100, *100*, 102–103, 106—*See also* Opiate receptors

117

Index

D

Dark matter 91, 93
DNA (deoxyribonucleic acid) *51*, 74, 109–110; *See also* Genes, Nucleic acids
Doppler effect 85
Douglass College 76, 79
Drug addiction 96, 99, 108
Ductus arteriosus (birth defect) 4, 5

E

Eckert, J. Prosper 29–30
EDVAC (computer) 30
Elementary Theory of Nuclear Shell Structure 22
Elements, chemical 17, 19–20
Elion, Gertrude Belle xi, xiii, xv, *48*, **48–58**, *53*, 61, 73, 74, 75, 79, 96, 109, 114
  acyclovir, development of 54–55
  antimetabolites, work with 50–51
  awards and honors 56
  azathioprine, development of 52–54
  chronology 57
  early years 49
  education 49
  further reading 58
  6-mercaptopurine, development of 52
  Nobel Prize 55–56
Endorphins 99–100, 102, 106
ENIAC (computer) 29–30
Enkephalin 99
Enrico Fermi Institute 19

F

Fallot, tetralogy of (birth defect) 4–5
Family life of women scientists—*See* Women in science—marriage; Women in Science—children

Fascists 16
FDA—*See* Food and Drug Administration
Fermi, Enrico 14, 16, 17, 19, 21, 41
Fission, nuclear—*See* Atoms—fission
Flowmatic (computer language) 31, 32
Fluoroscope 3
Food and Drug Administration (FDA) 9
Ford, Kent 87, 89
Fullerton, California State University at—*See* California State University—Fullerton

G

Galaxies 84, 87–88, 93—*See also* Andromeda; Dark matter; Spectra
  distribution 87
  motion 85, 88–91, 93
  structure 89–91, 93
Gallo, Robert 110–112, 116
Geiger counters 40
Genes 109–115—*See also* DNA; Nucleic acids
Georgetown University 86–87
"Glass ceiling" xii, xiii
Goldstein, Avram 96–97
Göttingen University 14–15, 40
Gout 54
Gravity, laws of 89–91
Gross, Robert 5
Grouper (fish) sex change 65

H

Harvard University 2, 27–29, 84
Heart 12
  birth defects 2–5
  surgery 5–7, 12, 54
Hemoglobin 3–4, 44
Heroin—*See* Opiates
Herpes viruses—*See* Viruses—herpes

119

Index

Hitchings, George 50, 52, 53, 56, 58
Hitler, Adolf 16, 17
HIV—*See* Viruses—AIDS
Hopper, Grace Murray xii, *26*, **26–37**, 62, 77
  awards and honors 35
  chronology 36
  compiler, development of 30–31
  early years 27
  education 27–28
  further reading 37
  languages, computer, work on 31–32
  Mark I computer, work with 28–29
  Navy, U.S., career in 28–29, 32–35
Hopper, Vincent 28
HTLV—*See* Viruses—HTLV
Hubble, Edwin 84
Hughes, John 99, 101
Hunter College 49, 61

I

Immune system 52–54, 95, 108, 111, 113, 114
Information, use of 34, 37
Insulin 96, 102
Iron (in hemoglobin) 44
Isotopes 17, 18

J

Jensen, Hans 22–23
Jews, persecution of 16
Johns Hopkins xi
  Mayer, Maria, at 15–16
  Pert, Candace, at 95, 98, 99
  Taussig, Helen, at 2, 3, 5, 7, 9

K

Kelsey, Frances 9
K-mesons 41
Kosterlitz, Hans 99, 101

L

Lady and the Sharks, The 65, 71
Lady with a Spear 60, 62, 67, 71
Languages, computer—*See* Computers—languages
Lasker Award 101, 106
LAV—*See* Viruses—AIDS
Lawrence, Ernest O. 40
Lee, Tsung Dao 41–42
Lenz, Widukind 7
Leukemia 52, 110–112
Limbic system *98*, 99–100
Los Angeles, California State University at—*See* California State University—Los Angeles
Los Angeles, University of California at (UCLA)—*See* California, University of—Los Angeles

M

"Magic numbers" 20–21
Manhattan Project 17, 40
Mark I (computer) 27–29, *28*, 30, 34
Marriage of women scientists—*See* Women in science—marriage
Maryland, University of 65, 68
Mass, missing—*See* Dark matter
Mauchly, John 29–30
Mayer, Joseph (Joe) xiv, 15–16, 18–19, 21–23
Mayer, Maria Goeppert xi, xiv, xv, *13*, **13–25**, 28, 39, 40, 41, 56, 84, 96, 109, 114
  atomic bomb, work related to 17–19
  awards and honors 23
  California, University of, at San Diego, years at 22–23
  Chicago, University of, years at 19–22
  chronology 24
  early years 14
  education 14–15
  further reading 25

Index

Index

Index

Index